T0347040

THE LITTLE BOOK OF HAMPSHIRE

ERICA WHEELER

*For Hilary Wheeler, my mother-in-law, born
and brought up in Hampshire and whose
father was one of the first to work on
Hampshire's motor torpedo boats.*

First published 2022

The History Press
97 St George's Place, Cheltenham,
Gloucestershire, GL50 3QB
www.thehistorypress.co.uk

© Erica Wheeler, 2022

The right of Erica Wheeler to be identified as the Author
of this work has been asserted in accordance with the
Copyright, Designs and Patents Act 1988.

British Library Cataloguing in Publication Data.
A catalogue record for this book is available from the British Library.

ISBN 978 0 7509 9957 1

Typesetting and origination by The History Press
Printed and bound in Great Britain by TJ Books Limited, Padstow, Cornwall.

MIX
Paper from
responsible sources
FSC® C013056

CONTENTS

INTRODUCTION

Hampshire is an intriguing county that rewards digging deeper. It is the heart of the ancient kingdom of Wessex, the maritime gateway to the world, and never really feels as far from the capital as its south-western neighbours. In fact it *was* the capital at one point. If you know where to find them, it has its own incredible archaeological sites, folk customs, royal riches, natural beauties, stories of seafaring (and airfaring!) and innovative industries. It is the home of air speed records, the medieval Treasury of the nation, three incredibly rare bat species, four royal weddings, the inspiration for a huge amount of writing, from Bibles to odes, and contains beautiful chalk grassland and heathland abundant with wild flowers and their attendant butterflies and dragonflies. Perhaps it hides its gems well but there are many of them. This book hopes to reveal a few of those rare and curious treasures.

It is the people of the county, past and present, which make it what it is, and this book profiles many of Hampshire's interesting but little-known personalities: monarchs, musicians, mothers, medics and eccentrics. They include Arts and Crafts artist-turned-archaeologist Heywood Sumner; the ultra-religious bestselling author Charlotte Yonge; the lord who became a train driver and race-winning motorist, John Montagu; the botanist and inventor of the first commercial motor-drawn caravan,

Richard St Barbe-Baker; and the expert horse rider who was also an academic geologist, megalithic monument builder and inventor of a 'tree-lifter', Colonel George Greenwood.

Places in Hampshire vary wildly: from the nineteenth-century seaside resort of Barton-on-Sea to the ancient Roman walls and amphitheatre at Silchester; from the harbour master's 'castle' at maritime Warsash to the bridge where St Swithun mended some broken eggs; from the octagonal Gothic library housing an incredible nineteenth-century book collection on China to the ancient Gospel Oak of Hampage Wood; from the prison hulks of Portsmouth Harbour to the water meadows of John Keats's poetry; and from the great transatlantic liners of Southampton Docks to Watership Down.

This book reveals the rich, hidden, unusual, rare and eccentric side of Hampshire, giving every reader a little something they didn't know about the county and encouraging everyone, whether born and bred in Hampshire or an inquisitive visitor, to explore this large and contrasting county. Given the richness of the county, there is so much more than I have been able to fit into these pages, so treat this as a stimulating but quirky taster of the wondrous place that is Hampshire.

1

WHAT IS HAMPSHIRE?

The county is fantastically diverse, encompassing acidic heathland and chalky downs, gin-clear streams and seaside piers, it is the recipient of invading ships and aircraft and the sender of fleets and armies. It is the home of royal cities and trading ports, the builder of seaplanes and warships, it is a grower of oaks, turf, watercress and vines. Is it possible to distil some of the things which make Hampshire uniquely Hampshire? This chapter tries to.

TIDE AND TIME

A quirk of tidal science has put Hampshire at the heart of south coast maritime life. Southampton Water famously has a 'double high tide', which makes it a boon to mariners. It results in a larger variety of times to sail in and out and unload. The resulting fast ebb tide scours the shipping lanes to make them deeper for shipping. The reasons are a complex mix of the Atlantic Pulse, numerous oscillations of the tide around the Isle of Wight and the shallower waters of Southampton Water.

Even the Venerable Bede in his *Ecclesiastical History* written in the 720s mentions it: 'In this sea, the two tides of the ocean … meet in conflict beyond the mouth of the river Homelea

[Hamble], which runs through the lands of the Jutes … and after this struggle of the tides, they fall back and return to the ocean whence they come.'

King Cnut, King of England from 1016 to 1035, is said to have tried to hold back the tide. There are several contenders for where this event took place, but one of them is Southampton. The idea was not to show he was omnipotent but because he knew he was not and wanted to prove so to his flattering courtiers. Upon failing and getting his toes wet, he announced that no man, even a king, is above God, for only He can control the tides.

However, the Solent has a tidal oddity that means the rising tide stops about two hours after low tide and begins again two hours after, officially called the 'young flood stand'. So had Cnut tried his trick at the 'young flood stand', he might have succeeded in suggesting the waters were being held back by his hand.

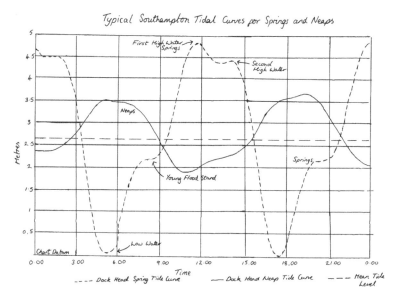

Typical Southampton tidal curve for spring and neap tides.
(Graph courtesy ABP Southampton Hydrographic Department)

Each year on the lowest tide of the year a cricket match is played on the exposed Bramble Bank in the Solent, usually just a navigational hazard. The Royal Southern Yacht Club and the Island Sailing Club play and take turns to 'win', as the game has to be rather short!

The Saxons divided the times of the day and night into eight 'tides', lasting three hours each. At Corhampton Church and Warnford Church you can see Anglo-Saxon sundials that show just this. Each line on the sundial indicates the midpoint of each tide.

In Warsash the clock tower rings 'ship's bell time', perhaps in deference to that village's maritime activities and its Maritime School. Many Hampshire sailors will have lived by ship's time. Ship's bell time divides the twenty-four hours of a day into four-hour watches, with one strike of the ship's bell made for the first half hour and another strike added for each half hour, until there are eight strikes for the end of the watch at four hours. There are two dog watches of two hours each between 4 p.m. and 6 p.m. and 6 p.m. and 8 p.m., allowing each watch to get eight hours' rest a night. Ship's bells have a long history and, a few miles away from Warsash, that of the *Mary Rose*, sunk in 1545, was one of the last items to be found on the Tudor wreck off Southsea.

SALT AND SMUGGLING

One of the less obvious things you can do with a seaside location is to make salt out of seawater. The people of Lymington made a very tidy, if seasonal, profit from it from the Middle Ages to the nineteenth century. The process consisted of first drawing seawater into clay-lined trenches where some of the water evaporated. The now concentrated brine was then pumped by windmills to tanks outside boiling houses where it was put into large copper boiling pans fired by coal. The salt crystals could then be skimmed off and dried.

The peak of the industry was around 1730, when eighteenth-century commentator Daniel Defoe said that all of southern England obtained its salt from Lymington and there were 163 pans in the Lymington area, exported all over the world. The last salt works in the country closed in Lymington in 1865.

Lymington also had another 'get rich quick' scheme, a rather more violent one – smuggling. It had a network of underground tunnels with which to get illicit goods from quay to a house or inn. But then this could be said of many places in Hampshire, both seaside and landward: 'I do not find they have any foreign commerce, except it be what we call smuggling, and roguing, which I may say, is the reigning commerce of all this part of the English coast,' said Defoe. In Hampshire there are many good beaches and inlets, less treacherous than in Cornwall and less guarded than in Kent, and a hinterland of the wild New Forest, almost untouchable by the excise men of old. As well as those that transported or landed the goods, there were others who turned a blind eye to the nocturnal transports. Kegs of brandy, bundles of silk and lace, tobacco and anything else that had a high tariff for the king were smuggled through.

One method of collecting smuggled goods while never being seen to go near the ships was to let the tide work for you. In Langstone Harbour, the barrels of spirits were set into the shallow water of the harbour on the flood tide, where an attached grapnel (or small anchor) would hold them in the beach as the water receded, ready for smugglers to collect.

Some souvenirs of smuggling in Hampshire:

- The table tombs in Boldre churchyard are said to have been the perfect hiding place for kegs of brandy, perhaps the first stop on from Lymington. Sway House Inn, Sway House and cottages were also said to be involved.
- The village of Cheriton was once well-known for its illicit trades in Hollands brandy, and the area of Brandy Mount remembers that.

- Soberton Church has a vault beneath the church near the chancel door and was perhaps to store contraband. It might have served as a smuggling route from Portsmouth to Medstead.
- Emsworth had easy access to the sea, making it another smuggling hotspot. It is said the Old Pharmacy in the High Street had a back room used for smuggling and an underground passage.
- Hamble, located on the river of the same name, was also a useful place for smuggling. A man called Sturgess apparently operated a very successful smuggling racket in the eighteenth century, gaining him enough profit to build a ship, a 20-gun cutter, the *Favourite*.

THE BIG BLUE

The southern damselfly is blue with a black mark like a spot with a large 'U' balanced on top, behind its wings. It is also very rare and the New Forest is one of the most important sites for it in the world. It is only found in the streams between Burley and Brockenhurst and between Lymington and Beaulieu and along the Itchen and Test rivers in Hampshire (as well as some in Dorset and Pembrokeshire).

Synonymous with Hampshire's areas of flower-rich chalk grasslands are the stunning blue butterflies: common blue, chalkhill blue, small blue, holly blue and the rare adonis blue and silver-studded blue (found in heathland), and the very rare large blue. Try Magdalen Hill Down near Winchester, a Butterfly Conservation reserve, in summer to see them.

Micheldever Wood, between Winchester and Basingstoke, remains one of the most beautiful bluebell woods in the country and is home to three species of deer and a variety of butterflies as well as prehistoric remains.

Hambledon Cricket Club, said to be the 'cradle of cricket' for its seminal additions to the rules and also their legendary run of wins in the 1770s, met in the Old Bat & Ball pub, next to the ground at Broadhalfpenny Down, before matches. What a sight they must have been – sky blue coats, with velvet collars, C.C. embossed on their buttons and gold-laced tricorne hats. The hats and coats were laid down when the match began and velvet caps worn for play.

Some women's sides, of which there were quite a few in the 1700s and 1800s, also wore blue. A cricket match was played in 1822 between Alresford 'matrons', playing in blue, and Alresford 'maidens', playing in pink. In both the original match and the return one, the maidens triumphed. There were also mixed matches in the 1700s. There is a record of a match between eleven women of Hampshire and twenty-two men of Hampton.

The Royal Navy wears navy blue and is known as one of the world's foremost 'blue-water navies', able to work globally and across deep oceans at long range. It has a long history in Hampshire and still has one of its three bases in Portsmouth. The first royal ships were commissioned by King Alfred the Great of Wessex and fought the first chronicled sea battle against the Vikings in 896 CE, although it didn't all go to plan. The heavier Saxon ships ran aground in an unnamed tidal inlet near the Solent and fought a bloody battle with the Vikings there. During the eighteenth century, Britain became supreme on the seas and the Admiralty expanded Portsmouth Dockyard enormously. By 1800 the Royal Dockyard at Portsmouth was the largest industrial complex in the world.

The Winchester Bible was the most ambitious, richly decorated, largest and most expensive Bible ever produced in the medieval period. It used an abundance of the colour ultramarine – a deep blue, even more difficult to obtain than gold leaf, found only in lapis lazuli from the mountains of Afghanistan. The Bible

Thresher shark. (Collage print by Ruth Ander)

was commissioned in the mid-1100s by Bishop of Winchester Henri de Blois, who had a taste for the finer things in life. It required 250 calfskins for the parchment of the huge pages, on which one monk took four years to write all the words. The illuminated and gilded letters and the pictures were made by six (probably travelling) artists. They were named (later) the Genesis Master, Master of the Apocrypha Drawings, Master of the Leaping Figures, Master of the Morgan Leaf, Master of the Gothic Majesty, and Amalekite Master.

Finally, there is blue in the sea too: lobsters. Found in the Solent, they look blue (before they're cooked) and even have blue blood. They can live for up to fifty years. Some more residents or visitors to the seas around Hampshire include the harbour seal and the thresher shark, an incredible beast that uses its long, curved tail to herd and stun its prey.

DRY DOCKS AND DRY WHITES

Construction of the first dry dock in the world was commenced on 14 July 1495 at Portsmouth Dockyard under the orders of King Henry VII and the design of Sir Reginald Bray. Two great gates were made and a 'middle dam' made of shingle and clay made it watertight. Then 120 to 140 men were employed for a day and a night to remove the water with an 'ingyn' – probably a bucket and chain pump worked by a horse gin. Getting the first ship, the *Sovereign*, out again took a little longer – twenty men took twenty-four days to remove all the clay and shingle and let the water in. It is thought to have been about 15m from where *Victory* lies today.

In 1895, exactly 400 years later, the fifth dry dock was opened at Southampton docks, the largest in the world at the time. Southampton went on to build two more, a total of seven, and a floating dry dock for the largest of ships.

Hampshire is a major producer of English white wines. The chalky sub-strata of the South Downs is almost exactly the same as the best Chardonnay vineyards in Champagne. The Romans grew vines in Hampshire and in the Domesday Book of 1086 there were forty-two vineyards listed. The revival in the 1950s of English-grown grapes started in Hampshire at Hambledon. In 1952, Major General Sir Guy Salisbury-Jones planted the first commercial vineyard there since 1875. The third vineyard opened was also in Hampshire at Beaulieu in 1957, owned by Lieutenant Colonel Robert. Today there are several vineyards and wineries, along the River Test and Itchen and still at Hambledon, making Hampshire an award-winning centre for English wine.

DOWNS AND DROWNERS

Hampshire's central section of landscape is largely made up of downs, which are really ups. That's because the word 'down' comes from the Celtic word 'dun' meaning hill. Hampshire's downs are some of the oldest grasslands in the country, some more than 3,000 years old, caused by centuries of sheep and rabbit grazing over chalk substrate. The downs are characterised by short springy turf and dry valleys, and an incredible variety of flowers and invertebrate life.

Notable downs include:

- Broadhalfpenny Down – cricket ground to Hambledon Cricket Club.
- Worthy Down – location of old Winchester Racecourse, haunt of King Charles II and major event on the social calendar of the 1700s.
- Magdalen Hill Down – now a butterfly nature reserve, full of wild flowers and wildlife, as well as the past site of a medieval leprosy hospital and a vast First World War camp.
- Beacon Hill and Seven Barrows – Lord Caernarvon is buried here and Geoffrey de Havilland, aircraft designer and manufacturer, built his first aircraft at Highclere and made his first flight from Seven Barrows field just below Beacon Hill.
- Watership Down – inspired the novel of the same name by Richard Adams.

Drowners aren't as bad as they sound, they worked in water meadows. Water meadows are a little more than just watery meadows. They are a joint venture between Hampshire nature and man. Nature provides the incredibly pure, constant and warm(ish!) 10°C chalk streams, by filtering rainwater through the chalk; and man, from the 1600s, built a complex system of water channels and ridges (called carriers, drains and panes) cut in the fields near the rivers. They are controlled by hatches and sluices, so water can flow through the field. This is not to water the crops at all, but to bring nutrient-rich waters and, perhaps most importantly, warm water to the land. The warm water, preventing frosts in winter, can produce a very early crop of grass and allowed animals to be fed through the winter more easily. It was labour intensive and dedicated 'drowners' maintained the channels of the water meadows to create the constantly flowing sheet of water. Hampshire contains nearly half of all water meadows in the country. Those south of Shawford are still working and you can see the ridges, furrows and sluice gates of old ones at St Mary Bourne and Winnall Moors, Winchester.

The Hampshire Down is also a breed of sheep that grazes on the downs and the water meadows. The Hampshire Downs, with their chalk grassland and chalk streams, made the sheep and the sheep made the Hampshire Downs with their grazing (and also were Hampshire Downs!). And the wool made Hampshire rich.

WATERCRESS AND SEAGRASS

Watercress is highly nutritious, with its leaves packed with vitamins C and A, calcium, folic acid and iron. Up to the 1940s there were over 1,000 acres of watercress beds across the country. Today 150 acres exist, concentrated in Hampshire and Dorset. Hampshire's clean-flowing chalk streams help the watercress to grow. Hampshire even has a railway line named after its salad vegetable: the Watercress Line, opened in 1865. It helped create the market for the easily perishable watercress as a nutritious crop of choice to Londoners, because the line ensured it could be quickly transported to Covent Garden and beyond. At its peak, watercress could be conveyed to Liverpool, via London Waterloo, in seven hours! Alresford became the centre

The spiny seahorse of the Solent has a fleshy 'mane' and uses its tail to wind around seagrass. (Collage print by Ruth Ander)

of the watercress industry with its station on the line and now is the centre of the restored steam heritage line (the only one in the county). It celebrates its heritage each year with the Watercress Festival in May.

Some of Hampshire's most extensive and wildlife-rich meadows are not high up on hills but under the sea. Seagrass meadows grow in the Solent's shallow waters and intertidal mudflats. One hectare of seagrass can support 80,000 fish and 100,000 invertebrates such as spider crabs and seahorses. Seagrass can also remove CO_2 from the atmosphere faster than even tropical rainforests! So they are worth protecting.

COMMONS AND COMMONERS

Commoners in the New Forest, numbering around 700, are landowners whose land to this day is associated with certain rights within the Crown forest. 'Common of pasture' results in New Forest ponies, cattle and donkeys grazing. But what are estovers, turbary, marl and mast? Common of estovers is a right to a supply of a certain amount of firewood; common of turbary is the right to cut peat turves (no longer exercised); common of mast is the right to turn out pigs in the autumn to devour the acorns; and common of marl is the right to dig clay to improve agricultural land (no longer exercised).

A rather different type of Commoner resides at Hampshire's only (but the oldest) public school (fee-paying and boarding), Winchester College. The school was founded in 1382 by Bishop William of Wykeham for seventy poor scholars. However, other fee-paying pupils soon joined them and became known as Commoners. Today Winchester College still has scholars, although many of them are not poor. They are, however, the most academic of the intake and are distinguished by their wearing of gowns and their special boarding house in the old 1300s buildings. Today there are over 600 Commoners. For the first time in nearly 650 years, girls were admitted in 2022.

Lord Eversley, or George Shaw Lefevre, grew up in Heckfield and later lived in Abbots Worthy House from 1896. He was connected to 'commons' in two ways. Firstly, he was a member of the House of Commons and a minister in Gladstone's government. Secondly, his real area of passion was the preservation of common lands. He actively sought to preserve commons for the benefit of the people. He wrote a book, *Commons, Forests and Footpaths*, founded the Commons Preservation Society in 1864 and fought enclosure. He also part-funded Eversley Park in Kings Worthy as a public recreation ground.

'Water has always been common,' ruled King Edward I in the Great Hall of Winchester in 1299 – meaning it is free for all to use. It was a ruling that came from a small-scale dispute of antisocial bullying in Winchester but was to have a far-reaching impact. Julianna was a laundress living in Upper Brook Street, Winchester, in the late 1200s. A working woman, she used the washing methods of the day – which involved washing clothes and fabric in great vats using urine. Her laundry business let out its waste liquids into the stream known as the Upper Brook, which still runs today, but now underground. A neighbour of hers, downstream, was the powerful and rich merchant John de Tytynge. He had a large house and was also mayor of Winchester in 1299 and 1305. Seemingly upset by her practice, he intimidated her and tried to block Julianna's access to the water of the brook. She complained that she should be allowed access to the water for her business. She eventually brought her case to the king at the Great Hall. The king ruled in her favour, adding, however, that the river should not be polluted, so that everyone could use it. He prohibited detritus from woad, called 'wodger', 'nor hides being tanned nor sheepskins nor blood nor waste of humans or animals, nor soiled infants clothing' from being put into the stream.

This might have remained a medieval footnote of an indomitable woman, but it also has relevance to our laws today. Julianna's Concord, as it was known, was the first statute law that obligated governments to protect natural resources, such as water, from pollution, for their people. It was used in drawing up the UN Convention of Human Rights and is used today in cases to bring government to account for polluted air. Those of us concerned with environmental issues owe Julianna de la Floude, as she became known, gratitude for her persistence!

Southsea Common is a large expanse of mown grassland along the shore from Clarence Pier to Southsea Castle. Its origin in the early nineteenth century was military: a clear range of fire was needed from the harbour defences towards any enemy ships that dared to approach Portsmouth and its dockyard. But at this time it was called the Great Morass and was a large and unsightly marsh. Convicts were employed between 1831 and 1843 to level and drain the common and it then became fashionable to ride around it from the developing seaside suburb of Southsea. The common is now a recreation ground, and serves as the venue for a number of annual events, including the Southsea Show, Kite Festival and Victorious Festival. Fans of Portsmouth FC gathered there to celebrate their victory in the 2008 FA Cup Final.

THROWSTERS AND FULLERS

Much of Hampshire's wealth in the Middle Ages was based on wool. Sheep were grazed on the downs and their wool was made into fabric at Winchester, where you might have found the following interesting but now obsolete things:

- Fulling mills – hammers powered by water wheels, which beat the fabric together with fuller's earth to clean and felt it.
- Tenter fields – where washed and dyed fabric was hung out tightly on tenter hooks to dry. Where we get the phrase 'on tenterhooks'.
- Teasel fields – the teasel plant seed heads were used to raise the nap of the finished fabric.
- Wool Staple – one of ten markets with an exclusive royal licence for selling wool from 1326 to 1363. Merchants from Lombardy, Flanders and Bordeaux gathered there (now Staple Gardens) to buy it.

A throwster would have worked in a silk mill, spinning silk thread. In 1766 a prohibition of imported woven silks and developments in weaving technology led to a boosted home-grown silk industry. Hampshire had silk mills in Winchester (first in St Peter's Street, then in Abbey Gardens), Overton and Whitchurch. The industry employed lots of women throwsters and children. Whitchurch mill produced silk for the linings of Burberry's clothes in the twentieth century. It also made silk for legal and academic gowns made by Ede & Ravenscroft. Whitchurch Silk Mill keeps the craft alive and still weaves silk today with wonderful names such as organzine, twill, ottoman, herringbone and striped satin.

Gabardine was a Hampshire invention, by Thomas Burberry, who opened a draper's store in Basingstoke in 1856. He invented a fabric inspired by the shepherds' smocks he saw, made of tightly woven linen to keep out the wind, and impregnated with their sheep's lanolin. Gabardine was water repellent and windproof and, crucially, it was breathable, unlike the rubberised rival fabric from Mackintosh. It became very popular with adventurers before the First World War. In 1908, Air Commodore Edward Maitland broke the record for long-distance air travel by flying from Crystal Palace to Russia in a

THE BURBERRY TRENCH - WARM

is made in the Burberry material referred to by Sir Ernest, and it is obvious that a cloth that can withstand the intense cold and gales of the Polar regions can be relied upon for protection and comfort under the scarcely less intolerable conditions of trench-warfare.

Whilst the outside of THE BURBERRY TRENCH-WARM is made in this wind-, rain- and snow-proof material, the inside is of luxuriously warm and soft Camel Fleece.

The coat is designed so that these two parts can be worn separately or together, thus supplying the services of three coats in one garment.

The outside alone, a Weatherproof that will turn any rain that an oilskin will; the Camel Fleece lining, a smart British Warm; and the two together the staunchest defence possible against the hardships inevitable in winter campaigning.

Officers' Complete Kits in 2 to 4 Days or Ready for Use.

Illustrated Naval or Military Catalogues Post Free.

An advertisement for the Burberry trench coat of 1917. (Courtesy Burberry) hot air balloon, 1,117 miles – wearing gabardine. Both Scott and Amundsen, racing to the South Pole in 1911–12 (and later Shackleton) used it, too. After his successful trek to the South Pole in 1912, Amundsen wrote to Burberry: 'Heartiest thanks. Burberry overalls were made extensive use of during the sledge to the Pole and proved real good friends indeed.'

In the First World War the Army used gabardine to make trench coats for over 500,000 soldiers. It became an iconic piece of outerwear, incorporating a check lining. Today Burberry is a worldwide fashion brand. Thomas Burberry died in 1926 and is buried at Holy Ghost Cemetery, Basingstoke. The showroom and workshop was on London Street, next to Deanes Almshouses, and the Burberry Emporium was in Winchester Street. The final Burberry factory in Basingstoke closed in 1957.

A HYTHE AND A HARD

A hythe is a place to land on a waterway, a jetty, and so is a hard – a gravelly bank to bring up your boat. With lots of watery and tidal inlets, Hampshire had a lot of these. However, two places, Hythe on Southampton Water and Buckler's Hard on the River Beaulieu, can tell you a lot about the industrial history of the county.

The history of Buckler's Hard could be summed up in four words: sugar, shipbuilding, steamers and sailing. It was first constructed to import sugar, then was a shipbuilding centre, then a destination for sightseeing Victorian steamers and finally today a haven for sailing yachts.

Buckler's Hard started life as the pet project of John, 2nd Duke of Montagu. This nobleman had inherited the estates of the former Beaulieu Abbey and with it immunity from paying harbour tolls and wharfage, and the privilege of owning the riverbed of the River Beaulieu. Added to this he was made the owner and governor of the West Indian islands of St Vincent and St Lucia by King George I. Put together, the duke realised he could import sugar from his own islands to his own port and set about developing Buckler's Hard. However, the settlement of St Vincent and St Lucia didn't go as planned to say the least and the project had to be abandoned.

The duke had a Plan B, however! In the 1740s he offered shipyard space at Buckler's Hard at a low rental with free timber. The shipwrights James Wyatt and Henry Adams came and many large ships were built there for the Admiralty. It is the only one of Hampshire's historic shipyards where buildings can still be seen today – a few cottages and Henry Adams's master shipwright's house.

Hythe, on the west side of Southampton Water, can be summed up in four phrases – sail, seaplanes, speed boats and hovercraft. It had made wooden ships in the Age of Sail but in 1911 Morgan Giles and May took over the shipyard and made yachts and early seaplanes. It was then bought by Supermarine, who also made seaplanes. It was later used by Supermarine's manager, Hubert Scott-Paine, and his new British Power Boat Company to make power boats – some of the fastest in the world – and motor torpedo boats for the Navy, which were fast, manoeuvrable craft to ambush enemy vessels. At this time Imperial Airways also leased part of the site for the maintenance of their flying boats, which ran flights all over the world from the Marine Air Terminal further up Southampton Water. After the British Power Boat Company folded in 1946 Hythe shipyard was taken over by Sir Christopher Cockerill for his Hovercraft Development Company.

MAST AND MASTS OR ACORNS AND OAK

New Forest ponies and pigs play a very important role in the upkeep of the ecosystem of the New Forest. The ponies' grazing of gorse and holly keep scrub at bay but surprisingly acorns are poisonous to them. Some ponies get a taste for acorns, however, and become very ill and die. Pigs are therefore introduced in autumn, the pannage season, under the commoners right of mast, to eat up the acorns, which they can do without harm.

Shipbuilding needs a vast amount of English oak, felled at between 80 and 120 years old, as well as considerable quantities of elm and beech. Although not for masts, actually! Fir, spruce or pine were needed for the masts and spars, and mostly imported from the Baltic and the Americas.

Shipbuilding began at Bursledon, Hamble and Southampton in the 1300s but the golden age of Hampshire shipbuilding was the age of sail, from about 1690 to 1820. As well as the Royal Dockyard at Portsmouth, Hampshire had shipbuilding yards at thirteen places: Bursledon, Hamble and Warsash (on the River Hamble); West Quay, Chapel and Northam (at Southampton); Redbridge and Eling (on the River Test); Bailey's Hard and Buckler's Hard (on the River Beaulieu); at Hythe (on Southampton Water), Lepe (on the Solent) and at Gosport.

In 1510 the *Mary Rose* took around 600 oak trees to make, but by 1765 *Victory* took around 5,500 trees. The New Forest was a source of timber for the royal dockyards. Regular inspections of New Forest trees were undertaken by the Navy and suitable shipbuilding trees were reserved and marked with the King's Mark, an upward arrow. These can still occasionally be found on oaks in the Forest today.

HANGERS AND HANGARS

Hampshire had an important pre-war aviation industry – alongside their hangars each factory had access directly to the … water! Strange though it seems to us, it was much more important to have a slipway to a long, calm stretch of water than a runway in those days. Seaplanes, which took off and landed on water, were the front runners in commercial aviation. Three historic hangars remain at Calshot – Sopwith, Sunderland and Schneider – forming the most outstanding group of early aircraft structures.

Airships were developed by the Army School of Ballooning at Farnborough in the early 1900s. Nearly all airship hangars have now disappeared but the Farnborough Air Sciences Trust still have the frame of a pre-First World War portable airship hangar, restored and re-erected. Their museum is housed in the old HQ for the Army School of Ballooning.

Hangers, in total contrast, are also a term for a distinctive feature of the landscape in eastern Hampshire – steep wooded hills. William Cobbett describes their beauty:

> The lane had a little turn towards the end; so that out we came, all in a moment, at the very edge of the hanger! And never, in all my life, was I so surprised and so delighted! I pulled up my horse, and sat and looked; and it was like looking from the top of a castle down into the sea, except that the valley was land and not water. Those who had so strenuously dwelt on the dirt and dangers of this route, had said not a word about the beauties, the matchless beauties of the scenery. These hangers are woods on the sides of very steep hills. The trees and underwood hang, in some sort, to the ground, instead of standing on it. Hence these places are called Hangers. From the summit of that which I had now to descend, I looked down upon the villages of Hawkley, Greatham, Selborne and some others.
>
> William Cobbett, 1822

CIVITATES AND VITAMIN C

What did the Romans do for Hampshire? Well, they built cities, collected taxes, began urban life, drained marshy areas, created central heating, built aqueducts and created a road network. A *civitas* was a large city and administrative centre of the Roman province of Britain, and Hampshire had two of them: Venta Belgarum and Calleva Atrebatum, known today as Winchester and Silchester. They were laid out with street grids lined with large houses (some with underfloor central heating, as seen in Winchester City Museum), shops and temples. Drainage works, defensive walls, water supplies and large public buildings, such as forums, basilicas and amphitheatre, were constructed. You can still see the amphitheatre today at Silchester, built to seat between 3,500 and 7,250 people who watched executions, wild beast fights (probably bears, bulls and wolves) and gladiator fights.

Conditions on board ships of the Navy in the 1700s were about as far as you could get from those early urban centres, there certainly wasn't much fresh water. Those from the Portsmouth slums were often 'imprest' into the Navy. One of the main scourges was scurvy, a terrible, painful, debilitating and ultimately fatal disease that afflicted sailors on long journeys, kicking in after around six weeks at sea. It was caused, we now know, by a lack of vitamin C. At one point during the Seven Years' War (1756–63) sailors were 100 times more likely to die of disease than be killed in action (that's 143 dying in combat and 13,000 by illness). Although Captain Cook gets the credit for trying to rid ships of scurvy, it is a Scottish-born doctor, working in Gosport, Hampshire, who actually made great leaps in understanding the disease with scientific methods. Dr James Lind, first working as a ship's surgeon then at the Haslar Naval Hospital, Gosport, conducted the first random control trials, concluding that citrus juice was the most efficacious in curing and preventing scurvy. The others in his trial were given cider or elixir vitriol or vinegar or seawater or a mixture of nutmeg, garlic, mustard and cream of tartar. Perhaps, needless to say, one major feature of medical trials today – informed consent – was absent from his methodology!

Ship's fever, actually typhus, was highly contagious and festered in unhygienic conditions where body lice passed it on. Lind observed this disease and insisted on scrupulous hygiene and immediate isolation of a suspected infection. Although living decades before germ theory emerged, his reflections on disease were prescient: 'The particles of contagion are of so subtle a nature, as seldom to fall under the inspection of our senses.' He also realised that, once on board ship, typhus could wipe out a crew, and therefore the best prevention was to make sure the crew were healthy before boarding. Easier said than done when recruiting from sailors just off another voyage or slum-dwellers. His work was pivotal in helping the Royal Navy gain supremacy in warfare.

MEN OF THE TREES AND GREEN MEN

There are several carvings of Green Men in Hampshire. The term is used to describe carved figures with foliage around them or sprouting from their mouths, ears or nostrils. Their origin is of some mystery, but they perhaps denote humanity's connection with nature and the wild. There are known examples in Winchester Cathedral's carved choir stalls and misericords, made in 1308, as well as an early one at Titchfield and one at Northington Church.

Green man carving on a misericord in the Quire of Winchester Cathedral.

Men of the Trees, known today as the International Tree Foundation, was founded by Sir Richard St Barbe-Baker (born 1889 in West End) to try to reforest parts of the planet. He was a botanist and environmental activist and grew up discovering the woods near his home at Beacon Hill. He was well ahead of his time and realised that deforestation was leading to soil erosion and natural disasters such as in America's dustbowl droughts of the 1930s. He helped reforest Kenya with the Kikuyu people in the 1920s. He died in 1982 in Saskatchewan, Canada. There is a plaque in West End village by Jill Tweed to this remarkable man and a street named after him. Today there are around 100 chapters of the Foundation and they have planted around 26 billion trees across the globe.

The Verderers are the council who manage the rights and usages of the New Forest. They hold the *Atlas of Forest Rights,* which details these, and are the last remnant of government administration called the Forest Government, which used to be common all over the country. There is evidence of the Verderer's Court from the thirteenth century. The court sat to hear cases of offences within the Sovereign's Forest and more serious crimes could be referred to higher courts such as the Forest Eyre. In the seventeenth and eighteenth centuries their role expanded to include protecting the growing of oak for shipbuilding, and by 1877 they became the guardians of common rights and the Forest Landscape. There are currently ten Verderers, who meet on the third Wednesday of each month at the Verderers Hall, Lyndhurst.

To be a member of the Old Green Bowling Club in Southampton is to play on the oldest bowling green in the world (established prior to 1299) and to be called an Old Green Bowler. The person who looks after the green is called Master of the Green. The club runs an annual bowling competition, the Knighthood Competition, which began in 1776 and is said to be the second oldest sports competition in the world. It has run continuously, despite a bombed bowling green in wartime, and the rules are slightly different from normal bowls. Previous winners are called Knights and cannot enter the competition again but they can be seen wearing top hats, tails and their medals to the competition. The players are called Gentleman Commoners and wear white. It has been known to take three weeks to find a winner but equally the contest can be over in one day!

The aptly named Colonel Greenwood of Brookwood, Bramdean, invented a 'tree-lifter' for transplanting trees up to 30ft in height with their ball of earth intact. The machine allowed a single individual to transplant one tree per day. The colonel was very enthusiastic about the importance of trees to the landscape and wrote a book in 1844 called *The Tree-lifter, Or a new method of transplanting forest* as well as *Rain and Rivers* (1857) and *Hints on Horsemanship* (1839). Through his interest in landscape gardening and hence soil erosion, he played a major role in reviving the geological theory of uniformitarianism and was adamant about the role of rain in valley formation. It was said in his obituary that 'had he fallen amongst geologists in early life, instead of amongst "thoroughbreds", he would doubtless have occupied a leading place among men of science'. An excellent horseman too, he also left an unorthodox memorial to his horse in Bramdean (see Follies in Chapter 9, Built in Hampshire).

An intriguing grotto in the woods near Cruxeaston is recorded in the 1730s. Built by nine sisters of the Lisle family from flints and decorated with seashells, it contained nine seats and a tenth for a 'presiding magician'. Perhaps this was Alexander Pope, who wrote a poem about the grotto and the nine ladies in 1733. One of the sisters, Harriet, was a talented artist and drew several pastel portraits of ancient family members and acquaintances. She placed them on the trees 'in a manner which produced a singular effect, as they appeared to form part of the trees themselves'. Only the grotto remained by 1804 and now even that has been taken back into the woods.

WIC AND WITAN

A shire is an Anglo-Saxon invention and Hampshire was one of the earliest shires, first mentioned in the *Anglo-Saxon Chronicle* in 757 CE. Before this time there were settlements, Roman cities, villas and roads, Iron Age hill forts, Bronze Age farms, but there were no shires and there was no place called Hamtun. Yet.

Hampshire, once formed, became the core of the powerful Anglo-Saxon kingdom of Wessex, the only one never to succumb to Viking rule. Winchester became the royal city of Wessex and essentially its capital, hosting the Witan or royal council, the state's treasure, the administrative centre, arts centre and royal palace. It also had the largest religious complex north of the Alps, was the largest fortified city or burgh, was the site of royal coronations, religious ceremonies and burials, was the main place for pilgrimage after St Swithun died in 863 CE and the centre of a rich bishopric. When the Kings of Wessex became so powerful they ran most of England in the 900s, Winchester became a capital of England. No wonder William the Conqueror hot-footed it straight to Winchester in 1066 in order to ensure his grand plan of finishing Anglo-Saxon resistance forever, and the Witan was no more.

Equally important, perhaps more so, was Hamwic, the Anglo-Saxon trading centre with its administrative centre, Hamtun, underneath modern Southampton. Wic is Old English for a trading and artisanal town. Lots of high-quality craft work and a huge amount of Anglo-Saxon coins have been found in archaeological work there. Hamtunscir was the area surrounding this Anglo-Saxon town and this place is, of course, what gave the county its name. In the Domesday Book it is called Hantescir, hence its shortened version is Hants. However, the shire reeve or sheriff was always based in Winchester, the ancient and current county town. Just to confuse matters, the county has also been called the County of Southampton or Southamptonshire for part of history: 1889 to 1959.

ALFRED AND *ANGELCYNN*

King Alfred the Great, King of Wessex (871–99 CE), was born in Wantage but made his principal city at Winchester. He was fourth of four brothers so never expected to be king, but he proved to be a very good leader. Under his reign a treaty with the Vikings was achieved, a system for defence of the kingdom rolled out (including fortified burhs at Winchester, Southampton and Portsmouth) and many churches were built.

He had a 'cultural programme' too: new art and scholarship was patronised and encouraged, especially at the Scriptorium in Winchester. Alfred himself may have translated some books from Latin to English. Alfred also had a vision to unite all the English people, the *angelcynn* in Old English or English kin, in one national cultural identity, even though they were at the time divided into several different political kingdoms. To this end the first *Anglo-Saxon Chronicle* was written in his court, probably at Winchester.

He is buried in the county, too – somewhere. He, his wife Aelswith and his son, King Edward the Elder, were reburied in Hyde, Winchester, in 1110, but the exact whereabouts have been lost (see Chapter 10, Lost and Found).

ANGELS AND ACANTHUS

Just after Alfred's time, in the 900s CE, a style of art was developed, the Winchester School, practised in the cultural and artistic centre of Winchester's three monasteries. It appears on illuminated manuscripts, carvings and other objects of art. Its hallmarks were the depiction of curling, draped fabric, foliage curled around birds and animals, heavy ornamentation, and lots of acanthus leaves, all in rich colours of purple, green, gold and blue.

One of the most exquisite and minute Anglo-Saxon finds in Winchester is a carved triangular piece of walrus ivory with two angels draped in fabric. It made up part of a small house-shaped shrine and it is a wonderful example of the Winchester School. It can be seen in Winchester City Museum.

The acanthus leaves and angels of the Winchester School can be seen in a much later work of art in Winchester Cathedral. Edward Burne-Jones and William Morris, a pre-Raphaelite artist and an Arts and Crafts practitioner, designed and made the stained glass of the Epiphany Chapel in 1910. The four windows depict the story of the epiphany in the Bible, including the annunciation that features an Angel Gabriel with stunningly coloured wings of deep magenta surrounded by acanthus-like foliage.

2

LAW AND ORDER

PRISONS

Winchester has had a gaol since at least the thirteenth century. The medieval gaol was located on Jewry Street (now a Wetherspoon's pub). A new building was constructed on Romsey Road in 1849 and employed the latest in prison construction theory, including: a radial design, based on the panopticon concept where gaolers could watch prisoners in all wings at all times from a central position; a good ventilation system utilising a central tower; and a treadmill for fifty prisoners and 'in-cell' hand cranks – boxes with handles to turn for no purpose other than punishment. The resistance of the handle could be increased by the warder by turning a screw, hence prison officers are known as screws even today.

There have been two attempted escapes from the prison. In 1909, Johan Witer escaped after attacking a warder with an iron bar. A massive manhunt ensued and he was arrested again after four days. Attempted murder was added to his crimes and ten years added to his sentence. Nearly 100 years later, another convicted murderer escaped in 2001 using a makeshift handsaw and a grappling hook and rope. He was also apprehended, though, and returned to the gaol.

The current prison has witnessed eleven public executions ending in 1868 and thirty-six private hangings before the death

The Warrior *hulk, from* The Criminal Prisons of London, and Scenes of Prison Life, Vol. 3 of The Great Metropolis *(1862) by H. Mayhew and J. Binny.*

penalty was abolished in 1965. The last triple execution in Britain happened at the prison on 21 July 1896. Three men were sentenced to death: Samuel Smith (found guilty of shooting his corporal at Aldershot Barracks), Philip Matthews (found guilty of murdering his 6-year-old stepdaughter in Portsmouth) and Frederick Burden (found guilty of murdering his girlfriend in Southampton) were taken to the gallows together and hanged at the same moment. The first execution in Britain carried out with the tolling of a bell instead of the raising of a black flag was at Winchester Prison on 22 July 1902.

There were up to twelve prison hulks – demasted and adapted boats – moored in Hampshire waters at Portsmouth, Gosport and Langstone harbours, including for a brief period the only one for female prisoners, HMS *Dunkirk*. These acted as prisons and as holding places for prisoners awaiting transportation. The prisoners were always on the lower decks, sometimes three decks down, chained in irons, and kept in dark, stinking conditions, with a high death rate: 'The universal depression of spirits was astonishing, as they had a great dread of this punishment,' said Duncan Campbell, who had responsibility for them.

Portchester Castle, together with the prison hulks, was used to hold French prisoners of war during the Napoleonic Wars – 8,000 of them. Conditions were bad, they ate the rats to keep from starvation and the West Indian soldiers suffered the worst from the cold and damp, many dying. The men passed the time by fashioning bones and wood into items such as dominoes, buttons, dice and playing cards, which they sold at a daily market. They also built a theatre, for an audience of around 300, putting on plays to professional standards, as some had trained in Paris. Local people were allowed in to see the performances until the theatre at Portsmouth complained. The theatre is reconstructed at Portchester Castle.

Francois Dufresne was remembered for his multiple daring escapes from Portchester and charismatic style. One time when he was in the Black Hole in the base of the keep, he fashioned a rope from his hammock, removed a stone from under the doorway and crawled out within feet of his guards, then let himself down the walls with his homemade rope. He made his way to London, navigating by the stars, and arrived at the French Agent's house saying, 'Give me some sort of a suit and a few sous to defray my expenses to the castle and I'll return and astonish the natives,' which he did! Shortly after this he was exchanged and returned to France.

GUNPOWDER, TREASON AND PLOT

Jack the Painter, aka John Aitken, was what we would call a terrorist today. He intended to cause great damage, through arson, with an ideology of republicanism behind his actions. He began his working life apprenticed to a painter, hence his soubriquet, and after being fired up with the ideas of American independence and republicanism in America, he hatched a plan to set fire to all British dockyards. He invented two types of 'infernal machines', to start fires, and in 1776 successfully set one off in Portsmouth Dockyard. One can imagine the inferno once the rope house, with its ropes and tar, was alight. It was brought under control eventually but not without severe losses. Jack was caught in Hook, with the incriminating evidence of a French passport, a bottle of turpentine and information about fireworks. He was tried (in Winchester) and sentenced to hang in a rather unusual way – from the mast of the ship *Arethusa*, 60ft high, by the main gate of Portsmouth Harbour. His corpse was tarred and hung in chains from Blockhouse Point at the mouth of the harbour.

Jack the Painter had a habit of turning up unexpectedly, though. It is said some sailors took down the body and took it to a tavern in Gosport. One can imagine the gruesome scene as Jack 'drank and smoked' with the hardened sailors. Apparently, the sailors got in trouble with money and were reduced to offering the bones of Jack the Painter to the landlord for their next drinks, which became the subject of a sailors' song ending 'Whose bones were some years since taken down, Were brought in curious way to town, And left in pledge for half a crown, Why truly Jack the Painter'. Jack also turned up again in 1891, this time just his finger. One of his mummified fingers, fitted as a tobacco stopper, was exhibited at the naval exhibition in Chelsea!

Another treasonous type who met a grisly end but had an afterlife in a Gosport venue was David Tyrie. He had been supplying the French with intelligence about the Royal Navy and its movements out of Portsmouth, at a time when it faced a threat from an overbearing France. Tyrie was found out while trying to convey his intelligence via packages on two separate occasions. He was charged with high treason and tried at Winchester Castle in the Great Hall in 1782. After a short, eight-hour hearing he was found guilty by the jury and sentenced to the terrible death of being hanged, drawn and quartered. He tried to avoid this with, firstly, a suicide attempt; secondly, by arranging an unsuccessful escape while being transferred; and thirdly, by tunnelling his way out of Winchester Gaol – all failed. He was the focus of intense anger and tens of thousands gathered to see his execution at what is now Southsea Common. Even after his death the mob tore open his coffin and hacked his body to pieces. One Buck Adams took his head, pickled it and displayed it as a curiosity in the Gosport Bridewell (prison).

Henry Garnet was an old Wykehamist, attending Winchester College in 1568. It was said he excelled at many things there including music and he was described as 'the prime scholar of Winchester College, very skilful in music and in playing upon the instruments'. How was it, then, that he ended up hanged, drawn and quartered on 3 May 1606? He had turned away from his funded place at New College, Oxford, and become a Jesuit priest on the Continent and then returned to England, run a secret Catholic press and taken over as Jesuit Superior in England after his predecessor was captured by the authorities. He heard about the Gunpowder Plot against King James I and his Parliament while hearing confession and so felt he could not reveal it. When the plot was found out, Garnet was arrested for knowing about it, interrogated, tried and sentenced to his gruesome execution.

One of history's greatest feats of legal argument and genius of oratory was the trial of Sir Walter Raleigh for treason in 1603 at Winchester's Great Hall. Although a favourite of Queen Elizabeth's, famously bringing back tobacco from Virginia, he had lost favour with King James I and was accused of plotting against the king by Baron Cobham. Due to the plague raging in London, Raleigh was brought to Winchester, among general hatred and anger from the common people. However, his performance in his trial utilised all his wit, intelligence and theatrics to turn the general feeling around and outdo and show up the vile prosecutor. 'Never was a man so hated and so popular in so short a time,' said Dudley Carlton of Raleigh, a commentator of the time. It is said he audaciously put English law on trial, using what we might call human rights arguments now. However much he gained new support, though, he was found guilty and sentenced to death. The sentence was not carried out, though, perhaps due to the new positive public opinion of Raleigh. He was taken to the Tower of London, alive but with the status of a dead man! His death sentence was carried out fifteen years later, as a political necessity after he had been released and attacked a Spanish fort in America.

William, Lord Russell, had a Hampshire seat at East Stratton. He was a strong supporter of the Exclusion Bill to exclude Roman Catholics from succeeding to the throne, including the then king's brother, James. He became involved in the Rye House Plot of 1683 to ambush the king and his brother. When discovered, he refused to flee to Holland as others did but was taken to the Tower of London and faced trial for treason. At the time no defence counsel was allowed when charged with treason, but unprecedentedly, his wife Lady Russell was allowed to act as his secretary. However, his guilt was a foregone conclusion and he was executed, although Charles II commuted the sentence from hanged, drawn and quartered to a simple and more merciful beheading.

Delours and Marian Pryce, sisters and members of the Provisional IRA, were the last people tried at Winchester's Great Hall, the incredible thirteenth-century castle hall that served as Winchester's law courts until the new court building was opened in 1974. They had been involved in a car bomb attack on the Old Bailey on 8 March 1973, which injured 200 people. They were found guilty and sentenced to life imprisonment, commuted to twenty years. They served only seven years before release in 1980.

FAKES, FORGERIES AND FUGITIVES

One of the most sensational and lengthy court cases of the Victorian age involved a small village, Tichborne just outside Alresford, and a case of identity fraud. It involved a man who claimed to be the heir to the Tichborne baronetcy, Roger

Tichborne. He had been thought dead in a shipwreck of 1854, but his mother believed he still lived, perhaps in Australia. Through advertising in Australian newspapers, a butcher from Wagga Wagga came forward, claiming to be her long-lost son. He was brought to England, his mother accepted him as her son, and his claim tried at court. He lost the civil case and was then tried in a criminal court for perjury. Some of the evidence against the claimant was as follows:

- Known as very thin in earlier life, this man was 400lb. Perhaps, it was thought, weight he had to put on to obscure his appearance.
- As soon as he arrived in England he called on an Arthur Orton, who he claimed was a very rich man now.
- His letters were full of spelling and grammar mistakes, although he should have been very well educated.
- He couldn't speak French, although Roger Tichborne was partly brought up in Paris.
- He didn't recognise his father's handwriting.
- He couldn't say what was in a package he had left behind before the shipwreck with a family servant.
- Prosecutors found lots of people willing to identify him as Arthur Orton, a butcher from Wapping.
- Roger Tichborne had tattoos that the claimant did not.
- His handwriting was analysed by a handwriting expert and matched Orton's not Tichborne's.
- He couldn't describe the ship that picked him up as a shipwreck survivor and brought him to Australia and the ship's log had no note of picking up shipwreck survivors.
- The prosecution had over 200 witnesses proclaiming him not to be Roger Tichborne.

Some evidence for his claim:

- Two family servants said they recognised him (although later recanted).
- His mother thought it was him and a couple of other family friends.
- He recognised family items such as favourite fishing tackle, favourite clothes and a family dog's name.
- He claimed the shipwreck had been very traumatic and scrambled his memory.

Despite campaigning throughout the country for support and the trial lasting 188 days, the longest-ever English court case at the time, he lost and was sentenced to fourteen years' imprisonment. It took the jury just half an hour to find him guilty. He died a pauper and was buried as such. However, the Tichborne family, rather tantalisingly allowed his coffin (and the death certificate) to read 'Sir Roger Charles Doughty Tichborne'.

Cartoon of Roger Tichborne and the Claimant comparing stature, Vol. 1 of the Tichborne Trials archive. (© 2021 Hampshire Cultural Trust)

Dame Alicia Lisle, a noblewoman aged 71, is known for being one of the first victims of Judge Jeffries's famous Bloody Assizes in Winchester and for the cruel sentence he gave her. She was accused of taking in fugitives from the Battle of Sedgemoor in 1685 and her husband's previous act of signing the regicide papers for King James's father, Charles I, didn't help her case. After essentially bullying the jurors into a guilty verdict, Jeffries announced a sentence of death by burning at the stake, immediately. Horrified, the Bishop of Winchester and other clergy intervened and it was postponed for five days and a plea with the king was attempted. The king would not commute the death sentence but did let the death be by the axe not burning. Spending her last night at what is now the Eclipse Inn, on 2 September 1685, she was beheaded in the Square in Winchester. An Act of Parliament later found the verdict was invalid as Judge Jeffries had obtained it by illegal means. It was too late for Dame Alicia Lisle. Her tomb is near the porch of Ellingham Church close to the family home of Moyles Court, with her daughter. But her story lives on in a painting in the House of Commons.

The Duke of Monmouth himself took refuge after the Battle of Sedgemoor, at Ringwood, where he was imprisoned. It was from Monmouth House, West Street, that he pleaded for his life with King James II, his uncle. The king was not disposed to save him and he hanged at Tower Hill.

Portals Paper, based in Laverstoke, made paper for the Bank of England. It was of the utmost importance that nobody got hold of the bank notes but also the special paper itself. It had a unique feel or 'handle' and watermark and could easily provide material for forging. The company has been responsible for technological innovations such as watermarks (from 1724) and security threads (from 1940). Security was also high at the factory and at Overton Station, where the wagons were chained and padlocked for transport.

However, the security was breached in 1862 with a heist involving several career criminals. A Harold Tremayne and his niece, Ruby, had arrived in Overton. She became engaged to a Mr Brown, who was then inveigled to obtain paper for them from the factory. A factory foreman, Mr Brewer, was also involved; he initially caught Brown but then joined them in the plot. They eventually led police to further 'paper handlers' in London: Edward Burnett and his associate 'Flash Emma', Mr Buncher, a butcher and Mrs Campbell, a known handler of stolen goods. James Griffiths, the mastermind of the scheme, was traced to Birmingham, where police seized the forger along with his tools and equipment. Griffiths had been obsessed with finding out the secret to the paper and having experimented with making it, gave up and arranged to steal it through this convoluted heist. Over 12,000 sheets of paper and £1 million in forged bank notes were found to be in circulation as a result of the heist – enough to have destabilised the British economy itself.

FOUR UNUSUAL TRIALS: DOUBLE JEOPARDY, DUELLING, AND ORDEAL

The last duel to the death between Englishmen on English soil occurred in 1846 in Gosport. Duelling by this stage was outdated and illegal, with the duellists as well as all witnesses and seconds liable to be tried for murder. However, in a matter of honour, Henry Hawkey of the Royal Marines Corps, and Captain James Seton, retired from the 11th Dragoons, faced each other on the deserted and remote Browndown near Gosport on 20 May 1846. Seton had been pursuing Hawkey's wife, and the insult to Hawkey's honour finally became too much. The duel resulted in Seton being shot in the belly. Taken to the Quebec Hotel (now Quebec House), he survived for seven days, but was then operated on by a London surgeon for internal bleeding and died soon after. Despite overwhelming evidence of their guilt, both the second, Edward Pym, and later Hawkey were found not guilty at Winchester Assizes, by juries taking just three minutes and barely a second, respectively, to return their verdicts. Hawkey became the hero of the hour, cheered in the streets of Winchester as he passed and even the judge was 'saluted … with hearty huzzas'.

For 800 years in English law, a defendant could not be tried a second time on the same (or similar) charges after they had been acquitted, under a principle called double jeopardy. But the law was changed in the 2003 Criminal Justice Act to allow the Court of Appeal to quash an acquittal and order a retrial when 'new and compelling' evidence is produced. One of the first double jeopardy cases was heard in Winchester for the brutal murder of Georgina Edmonds at Brambridge in 2008. Matthew Hamlen had been found not guilty of the crime, but when Detective Inspector Chudley re-examined fibres and found new DNA evidence Hamlen was able to be retried and this time in 2016 found guilty. The judge, Mr Justice Saunders, said to the jury members, 'It is an experience that will live with you for the rest of your lives,' and each jury member, if they wished, would be exempt from jury service for the next ten years.

Emma was an Anglo-Saxon queen, twice over. She was the only person to be married to two Kings of England and be mother to two Kings of England. She was married firstly to King Aethelred the Unready (in 1002) and gave birth to Edward (later the Confessor). When Aethelred died, she married the new King from Denmark, Cnut (in 1016), and had a son with him, Hardacanute. But she was also subject to a scandal in her later years. She was accused by her son, Edward the Confessor, of some 'inappropriate behaviour' with the Bishop of Winchester, Alwine (despite the fact he had died three years earlier!). In order to prove her guilt or otherwise, she was to undergo trial by ordeal. Rather than evidence, witnesses and deliberation by a jury, this was a type of trial used by the Anglo-Saxons where God determined the outcome. Here the accused must undergo an 'ordeal' and see if they are saved by it, thus proving their innocence. In Emma's case, she was ordered to walk barefoot over nine red hot ploughshares in the Old Minster of Winchester. After praying all night to St Swithun, and receiving a reassuring message from him, she duly undertook the trial and was unhurt! She got to reprimand her own son, and he was whipped by both her and the other bishops who accused her.

Thomas Boulter's immortal line was 'your money or your life', as recorded in his trial for highway robbery in 1778 at Winchester Assizes in the Great Hall. He was a prolific highwayman, threatening his victims on the turnpike roads of Hampshire with his brace of pistols but never actually hurting anyone, as he pleaded when found guilty and sentenced to hang. Good looking, confident, always with a ready story and charming manner, he robbed on the Salisbury to Stockbridge road, and also at Basingstoke, Romsey, Nursling, West Meon. He always acted with politeness and even an apologetic manner while undertaking his 'felonious and violent assaults', as the court termed it. He moved on to the north, where he was actually caught, charged and sentenced at York. But he was reprieved if he would join the Army. He did this, but within a week had deserted and persuaded, in his inimitable style, a guard on the Bristol stagecoach to take him south. Here he teamed up with a James Caldwell and continued his criminal exploits. However, he was caught again in Birmingham and yet again escaped. He decided to make for the Continent but the war with France had closed all the ports. He was eventually caught again and tried at Winchester. He charmed his way into being allowed to write his memoirs before execution, but there was no reprieve this time. He was hanged at noon, on 19 August 1778.

3

SPEED: CONQUERING THE ELEMENTS OF SEA AND AIR

The Schneider Trophy is an international award for flying the fastest in a seaplane. It was won at Calshot, Hampshire, in Hampshire-made planes three races in a row (1927, 1929 and 1931). The trophy consists of a nude winged figure kissing a zephyr recumbent on a breaking wave. The heads of two other zephyrs and of Neptune, the god of the sea, can be seen surrounded by octopus and crabs. The symbolism represents 'speed conquering the elements of sea and air'. Hampshire has a history of doing just that.

FIVE MEN LIVING IN THE AGE OF SPEED

Five men living and working in Hampshire, born in a twenty-five-year period, had remarkable lives in the era of 'speed', mastering virtually every mode of powered transport between them.

Samuel Cody
Born: 1867
Lived: Born in Iowa, but lived and worked at Farnborough in the early 1900s.
Early life and escapades: Started as a Wild West showman, in Forepaugh's Circus, much like Buffalo Bill Cody, with whom he is often confused.

First foray into speed: He became interested in kites, developing a double-cell box kite capable of flying at high altitudes and carrying people. They were used for weather observations and he became a fellow of the Royal Meteorological Society. The Admiralty became interested in the kites, which could be used for observations even in windy weather, and ordered four of Cody's War-kites. He then became Chief Instructor of Kiting at the Army School of Ballooning in Farnborough and his kites were officially adopted for the Balloon Companies of the British Army.

In 1905, using a radically different design looking more like a tailless biplane, he devised and flew a manned 'glider-kite'.

Main claim to fame: His flight in his self-designed British Army Aeroplane No. 1 of 16 October 1908 is recognised as the first official flight of a piloted heavier-than-air machine in Great Britain. On this date he tied his plane to a tree at the Royal Aircraft Factory, Farnborough, ran the engine up to full power and then signalled for the ropes to be released. He flew about 200 yards before landing and put himself and Farnborough in the history books.

Sidelines in speed: On 5 October 1907, Britain's first powered airship, developed by Cody, British Dirigible No. 1 *Nulli Secundus*, flew from Farnborough to London in three hours twenty-five minutes, with Cody and its commanding officer, Colonel J.E. Capper, on board.

Samuel Franklin Cody. (Courtesy Farnborough Air Sciences Trust Museum)

Other notes: He continued to work on his own planes until his death in 1913 in a crash in his own plane, the Cody Floatplane, at Laffan's Plain, Farnborough. Cody was buried with full military honours in Aldershot Military Cemetery, when the funeral procession drew an estimated 100,000 people. A replica of Cody's British Army Aeroplane No. 1 was made in 2008 and can be seen at the Farnborough Air Sciences Trust Museum. There is also a statue of him close by.

John Scott Montagu of Beaulieu

Born: 1866

Lived: Palace House, Beaulieu, New Forest.

Early life and escapades: When he was 15 he sneaked out of Palace House at dawn, walked to Buckler's Hard and took his dinghy for a jaunt around the entire Isle of Wight. He made a triumphant return at 11 p.m.

First foray into speed: After Eton and Oxford, John, Lord Montagu, signed up as an apprentice at the London & South Western Railways' Nine Elms locomotive depot. He learnt about the work-ings of steam locomotives and became a qualified engine driver.

Main claim to fame: Early campaigner for motoring. He entered the Paris–Ostend 1899 race, finishing third; in 1900 he took part in the Thousand Mile Trial around England, where he was one of thirty-five to finish the race of sixty-five entrants. He introduced the royal family to motoring, taking the Prince of Wales for a drive. As MP he helped to introduce compulsory number plates and the raising of the speed limit to 20mph. He also introduced a bill to make a high-speed road between London and Liverpool, only realised with the first motorway in 1958.

Sidelines in speed: He raced an early power boat, *Napier II*, winning the British International Trophy in 1905.

Other notes: He founded one of the first motoring magazines, *The Car Illustrated*, a beautifully illustrated periodical, subtitled *A Journal of Travel by Land, Sea and Air.*

Lord Montagu also had a run-in with a sinking ship, although not in Hampshire. The boat he and his mistress were sailing on was torpedoed by a German U-boat in the Mediterranean in 1915. Eleanor, his mistress, was killed and Montagu was rescued after thirty-two hours in the water. He became one of the only people to read his own obituary in the papers.

As well as his advocacy of all things with an engine, he was, in contrast, a Verderer of the New Forest (see Men of the Trees and Green Men in Chapter 1, What is Hampshire?), in which his Beaulieu estate sat.

Thomas Sopwith
Born: 1888
Lived: Latterly in King's Somborne.
Early life and escapades: On holiday in Scotland with his family aged 10, a gun lying on his lap accidentally went off, killing his father, an event that haunted him his whole life.
First foray into speed: He was an expert ice skater and a member of the national ice hockey team. He experimented with: motorbikes, for which he won a medal for a 100-mile trial in 1904; ballooning, which he tried in 1906 and then bought his own balloon; and cars, which he started a business selling in London.
Main claim to fame: He founded the Sopwith Aviation Company and they produced more than 18,000 aeroplanes for the Allies in the First World War, including over 5,000 single-seat Sopwith Camel fighters. His first flight was on 22 October 1910, which ended with a crash after about 275m, but he soon improved and on 18 December 1910 he won a £4,000 prize for the longest flight from England to the Continent in a British-built aeroplane, flying 169 miles in three hours forty minutes. He used the winnings to set up the Sopwith School of Flying at Brooklands and in 1912, with partners, the Sopwith Aviation Company. Bankrupted after the war by punitive taxes and a failed motorcycle venture, he started a new aviation business, Hawker Aircraft, in 1920.

Sidelines in speed: He also competed with yachts, entering the Americas Cup twice, in 1934, when he went down in legend by nearly winning it, and in 1937. Portsmouth company Camper & Nicholson designed his Americas Cup yachts and his own luxury motor yachts.

Other notes: A flypast of military planes over his home at Compton Manor, King's Somborne, was organised for his 100th birthday. He died there on 27 January 1989 and is buried in All Saints Church, Little Somborne.

Edwin Alliott Verdon-Roe

Born: 1877

Lived: He lived at Hamble House from 1929 until 1940 and is buried at Hamble Church.

Early life and escapades: Left home at 14 to train as a surveyor in Canada but had to resort to odd jobs for a year before coming home. He trained as an apprentice at the Lancashire & Yorkshire Railway, and then worked in the Merchant Navy as an engineer. He became inspired by albatross and made his own gliding models on his last voyage in 1902.

First foray into speed: He won a *Daily Mail* competition with his aircraft design and with his £75 prize money began to build a full-size plane, the Roe I biplane. He was the first Englishman to fly in England in an English-designed and -made plane. This he did on 13 July 1909.

Main claim to fame: In 1910 he founded the Avro Aircraft Company and his most successful model was the 504, which sold more than 8,000 to the Royal Flying Corps and RAF and was made in Hamble from 1916 to 1919.

Sidelines in speed: He later bought an interest in Saunders, making it Saunders-Roe (or Saro). They made a huge number of floating and flying machines, including the first jet-powered flying boats, the Skeeter helicopter, the Princess seaplane airliner (see Chapter 5, Disasters) and even Britain's only rocket programme (later abandoned) from their bases in the Isle of Wight and Eastleigh airport. His grandson, Bobby, born in 1965 in Winchester, is a professional racing car driver.

Hubert Scott-Paine
Born: 1891
Lived: In Bitterne, set up factories in Woolston and Hythe.
Early life and escapades: He worked selling yachts with Noel Pemberton-Billing and the two started up Supermarine Aviation Ltd. He bought out Pemberton-Billing in 1916.
First foray into speed: With excellent foresight he employed the very talented R.J. Mitchell (designer of the Spitfire) at Supermarine Aviation in 1917. They then set about designing super-fast seaplanes to compete in the Schneider Trophy. Unsuccessful in 1922, Supermarine planes won in 1927, 1929 and 1931.
Main claim to fame: Scott-Paine is famous for not one but three Hampshire businesses that he led. Firstly, Supermarine, later maker of the Spitfire. Secondly, his pioneer work in developing

One of the first motor torpedo boats on its voyage along Southampton Water to its commissioning ceremony for the Navy in 1936. Netley Hospital is in the background. A newspaper said: 'The M.T.B. – the sun glistening on her freshly painted hull, a delicate Mediterranean grey – presented a beautiful picture as her sharp bow cleaved the water and flung the spray back in her smooth and speedy progress down the waterway.' It was 'expected to revolutionise naval warfare in narrow waters'.

commercial passenger seaplane travel, first from Southampton to the Channel Islands and Le Havre and then merging his company to create Imperial Airways, which took passengers, using seaplanes, all around the world, for the first time. Thirdly, he created the British Power Boat Company at Hythe, which developed innovative world water speed record-beating power boats and motor torpedo boats for the Navy.

Sidelines in speed: He piloted power boat *Miss Britain III* himself in Hampshire waters and was the first to break the 100mph barrier in a single-engine boat.

INCREDIBLE VEHICLES THAT WERE 'BORN' IN HAMPSHIRE

Ships

HMS *Agamemnon*. This was a 64-gun third-rate ship built at Buckler's Hard by the shipbuilder Henry Adams and launched in 1781. She was Admiral Nelson's favourite ship and he captained her from 1793 for three years. She had an eventful life when 'Britannia ruled the waves' taking part in the American Revolutionary War, the French Revolutionary War and the Battle of Trafalgar, as well as being caught up in the mutinies at Spithead and Nore in 1797, before escaping from the hardcore mutineers. She took a major role in the Siege of Bastia and Calvi in Corsica where Nelson lost his right eye, had a great fight with the much larger French 100-gun ship *Ca Ira,* and accompanied Nelson at the Attack of Santa Cruz, where he lost his right arm. Her crew, not approving of the naval fashion for classical names, took to calling *Agamemnon* 'Eggs and Bacon' (HMS *Bellerophon* became 'Billy Ruffian' and HMS *Polyphemus* became 'Polly Infamous' at the same time). *Agamemnon* ended her days grounded at the entrance to the River Plate in South America. In Patrick O'Brien's popular series of books, *Master and Commander*, Jack Aubrey serves as lieutenant on the *Agamemnon* before the action of the first book takes place.

HMS *Implacable*. Portsmouth Historic Dockyard is famously home to the *Victory*, Nelson's flagship at the Battle of Trafalgar and one of the nation's and the Navy's treasures. But Portsmouth was also home until relatively recently to one of her great French adversaries, what was the *Duguy Dumanoir* but became HMS *Implacable* once it was captured from the French. In fact, she fired the shot that tore off the topsail on Nelson's ship. Once captured she served in the British Fleet, then was fitted as a training ship and towed into Portsmouth Harbour in 1932 – the two battleships seeing each other for the first time in 127 years. All the warships dipped their flags in greeting. She was finally scuttled in the 1950s by blowing her up in the Channel with British and French flags flying, although it took two attempts.

Pandora. This was a Buckler's Hard-built ship launched in 1779, with a dramatic life story. She was sent out in search of the *Bounty*, whose crew had mutinied and cast Captain Bligh adrift. The *Pandora,* captained by Captain Valentine Edwards, discovered fourteen of the mutineers at Tahiti and arrested them. They were placed in a makeshift prison on the quarterdeck nicknamed 'Pandora's Box'. However, *Pandora* was wrecked off Australia on the home voyage in 1791 and all prisoners were in danger of drowning. One seaman, however, saved most of them by freeing them from their irons.

MTB 71. Hampshire has also been a centre for making power boats and yachts. Vosper, based in Portsmouth, and the British Power Boat Company developed motor torpedo boats. In the Second World War they were fast, small boats able to enter inaccessible waters in secrecy and escape with agility, part of the Navy's Coastal Forces. They were also known as Night Hunters or Spitfires of the Sea. Their crews won the highest number of medals for gallantry in the war. The last one in existence is *MTB 71,* found being used as a houseboat. It has been restored and is now displayed at Explosion Museum of Naval Firepower in Gosport. Vosper also made the *Bluebird K4*, which took the world water speed record at 141.7mph on 19 August 1939, driven by Sir Malcom Campbell on Lake Coniston.

Miss England I and *Miss Britain III*. These were both made at Hubert Scott-Paine's British Power Boat Company at Hythe to contest the world water speed record. Miss England was made in 1928 and took the world water speed record at 91mph in America, driven by Harry Segrave (incidentally on the same trip to America in 1929 Segrave took the world land speed record in Golden Arrow, now on display at the National Motor Museum at Beaulieu). *Miss Britain III* was a revolutionary design, covered in aluminium, the absolute epitome of its art deco age. It was developed in great secrecy and tested at dawn on Southampton Water. It competed in the Harmsworth Trophy of 1933 in America, losing narrowly.

Deo Juvante II. This was a motor yacht made by Camper and Nicholson in Portsmouth, was one of several boats of note made by them. Previously a mine hunter, it made three runs across the Channel in the Second World War Dunkirk evacuation and was then bought by Aristotle Onassis and given as a wedding gift to Rainier III, Prince of Monaco, when he married actress Grace Kelly. It was used for their honeymoon, cruising the Mediterranean.

'Berthon' folding lifeboat. This was a rather different type of craft. It was designed as a space-efficient lifeboat, so that enough could be carried on ships to save everyone. Rev. Edward Lyon Berthon, vicar at Romsey Abbey and curate of Lymington, was inspired by the loss of 100 lives on the SS *Orion* due to a lack of lifeboats. He designed a lifeboat in 1851 with a series of Canadian Elm wooden ribs on either side of a strong keel. Between these ribs were flexible double-skinned canvases coated with a secret mixture to add water resistance. Once opened, the canvas folds stretched into multiple, air-filled, watertight compartments to give the boat buoyancy. They were easily stowed, easily launched and easily repairable. Queen Victoria was a fan, though the Admiralty took a while to be convinced, but eventually they were a great

An advertisement for Berthon folding boats. (Courtesy Berthon Boat Company Ltd)

success. Berthon also built a folding bandstand and marketed a pontoon-bridge kit to the military, utilising the folding boats. They were built in Romsey and then the Lymington Shipyard, where the company can still be found today running a successful boatyard, marina and yacht brokerage.

AEROPLANES

Spitfire. In 1919 Supermarine in Woolston hired R.J. Mitchell as its Chief Designer and began to design flying boats. After success and a huge learning curve with innovative designs for the Schneider Trophy (see below in Is It A Boat? Is It A Plane? Flying Boats, Seaplanes and Airships), Supermarine designed the first Spitfire. It would become an iconic plane during the Second World War.

Horsa. The earliest action on D-Day was by a small number of troops who glided behind enemy lines shortly before midnight and landed undetected to take a bridge over the Caen Canal (now Pegasus Bridge) and one over the Orne River (now Horsa Bridge). Those gliders, called Horsas, were designed by the Airspeed company based at Eastney, near Portsmouth. Gliders had the advantage of landing troops together, rather than scattered by parachute, and quietly. One is exhibited at the D-Day Museum, Southsea. Unfortunately, one crashed near Warnford in 1944 during D-Day preparations, killing the twenty-seven on board.

The Southampton University Man Powered Aircraft (SUMPAC). This became the first human-powered aeroplane to make an officially authenticated take-off and flight, on 9 November 1961. Its longest journey was 594m at a height of 4.6m. Pedals and chains drove a two-bladed propellor to power it. It was designed and built by Southampton university students between 1960 and 1961 for an attempt at the Kremer Prize, although it never completed the course.

Gnat. Folland Aircraft was based at Hamble and produced the 'Folland Frightful' (from its unusual appearance), the Midge and then the Gnat, famously used by the Red Arrows display team and 'a masterful piece of economical design' – much more lightweight than the fighters that had gone before.

IS IT A BOAT? IS IT A PLANE? FLYING BOATS, SEAPLANES AND AIRSHIPS

S5 and S6 seaplanes. Rather boring names for extraordinary planes: they were revolutionary designs for extreme speed in order to win the international Schneider Trophy, which had become a matter of national pride. They were made by Supermarine in Woolston. Meanwhile, Calshot, at the western mouth of Southampton Water, became the home of the High Speed Flight or just The Flight, a group of ace airman who would compete in the planes. The waters off Calshot became the scene of some of the most exciting inter-war air races of the Western world. The contest was set up by a French flight enthusiast, Jacques Schneider, and ran between 1913 and 1931 with laps over a (usually) triangular 220-mile course. Some of the contests attracted crowds of over 200,000 spectators. According to the rules, if the Schneider contest was won three times in a row by one country, then they held the Trophy in perpetuity. Britain won it in 1927 in Venice, in 1929 in Calshot and again in 1931 in Calshot (although this was a walkover as no other nation entered that year) and therefore won the trophy forever. It can be seen in the Science Museum, London. After the race, speed records were also set when Flight Lieutenant Stainforth then achieved a record of 407.5mph, the first person to travel faster than 400mph. The original S6A can be seen at the Solent Sky Museum in Southampton.

The Mayo Composite plane. This was actually two aircraft, one stuck on top of the other. From 1937, Imperial Airways flew from Southampton all over the British Empire in their flying boats; however, in reality the flights were made in short hops.

To increase the range of the planes, a 'composite' aeroplane was devised – this comprised the four-engine floatplane Mercury (landing on narrow floats under the body of the plane) mounted on top of a flying boat Maia (which lands on its hull). Maia would use fuel to take-off and climb to altitude, then release Mercury from the top of it, to complete the flight. The combination would allow a full mail load to be carried 3,500 miles even against a headwind. It looked strange and one wouldn't believe it could get off the water. But it did!

PB7. Just before the First World War, Supermarine received an order from the German Navy, which for obvious reasons couldn't be completed. It was to be a flying boat called PB7, which could shed its wings when on the water and turn into a motor boat, reminiscent of something from James Bond. Other Supermarine designs were a scout biplane called the Seven Day Bus because it could be built in that number of days, and the Nighthawk, an eccentric quadruplane for attacking Zeppelins.

SRA/1. Do the words jet fighter and seaplane naturally go together? Not really. But that's just what Saunders-Roe did in 1947, when they designed the SRA/1, the world's only jet fighter flying boat. Designed to operate even without airbases, only three were made, one of which is now in the Solent Sky Museum, Southampton, but the end of the war in the Pacific meant they were no longer considered necessary.

Nulli secundus (meaning second to none). This was the first airship developed at Farnborough School of Ballooning by Samuel Cody. The dirigible was made of fifteen layers of goldbeater's skin, a material made from calf intestine membrane, valued for its resistance to tearing, and a long triangular-section framework of steel tubing, suspended by four silk bands. It was powered by a 50hp (37kW) Antoinette engine driving a pair of two-bladed aluminium propellers via leather belts. *Nulli Secundus II* was also built at Farnborough's Balloon Factory, although the name began to sound preposterous (it translates

The Nulli Secundus II *airship, flying in 1908. (Courtesy Farnborough Air Sciences Trust Museum)*

as second to none the second). It had a new silk outer skin and a revised understructure. It flew in July 1908 before a crowd of thousands but was scrapped by the end of 1908.

Hovercraft. A hovercraft is a bit like a boat and a bit like a plane; even the driver is called a 'pilot' and driving it is called 'flying' – but it travels on water. It was initially regulated by the Civil Aviation Authority but now the Maritime Coastguard Agency – they can't quite make up their minds. The hovercraft can be said to have its home in Hampshire for four reasons: 1) the longest-running and oldest commercial hover port, run by Hovertravel, is at Southsea, in operation since 1965. It operates between Southsea Common and Ryde, Isle of Wight, and at ten minutes is the fastest route across the Solent; 2) Sir Christopher Cockerell, the inventor of the hovercraft, lived and developed his hovercraft at Hythe, following his kitchen table experiment using two tin cans and a hoover; 3) new technologically advanced hovercraft are today developed at

Southampton by Griffon Hoverwork; 4) Lee-on-the-Solent has the Hovercraft Museum, including the earliest models trialled in Southampton Water and a hovercraft made from a Mini car!

AND EVERYTHING IN BETWEEN …

The 'Winchester' caravan by Hutchings, based at Winchester, was a streamlined marvel and a very popular model in the golden age of caravanning. It dominated the industry for decades. It was made by Bertram Hutchings, who started designing horse-drawn caravans before the First World War and he and his family spent virtually half the year on the road, where he also pursued his passion of photography (of which he was so accomplished he could have been a professional). This renaissance man was also extremely musical and an expert organ player!

The Navarac caravan was the first commercially produced trailer caravan designed to be pulled by a motor car and was the design of Captain Richard St Barbe Baker (a Hampshire native, born at West End), utilising spare aeroplane parts after the First World War. The caravan was built on an aeroplane undercarriage with four wheels, and featured a lantern roof, little windows and a stable door. The Navarac took its first outing in May 1919. It was in much demand and had a virtually 100 per cent profit margin. St Barbe Baker couldn't lose! Or could he? Once it was exhibited at Olympia, other businesses overtook the company with new designs. St Barbe Baker went back to focusing on his first passion of forestry (see Men of the Trees and Green Men in Chapter 1, What is Hampshire?).

In 1958, Peter Chilvers, as a young boy on Hayling Island, assembled his first surfboard combined with a sail. In a court case of 1982, Chilvers's board was recognised as 'prior art' as it incorporated all the elements of a modern windsurfer. The courts found that later innovations were 'merely an obvious extension' of Chilvers's board, which he had backed up with film footage.

INTRIGUING 'SPEED' COLLECTIONS IN HAMPSHIRE

- Hovercraft Museum, Lee-on-the-Solent
- Solent Sky Museum, Southampton
- National Motor Museum (NMM)
- Shell Heritage Art Collection (at NMM)
- Motoring Archive (at NMM)
- Motoring Object Collection (at NMM)
- Motoring Picture Library (at NMM)
- Caravan and Motorhome Club Collection (at NMM)
- Army Flying Museum, Nether Wallop
- Royal Navy Submarine Museum, Gosport
- Portsmouth Historic Dockyard
- Buckler's Hard (old shipbuilding village)
- The Diving Museum, Gosport
- Explosion Museum of Naval Firepower, Gosport
- Sea City Museum, Southampton
- Milestones, Basingstoke (including transport collection)
- Watercress Line, heritage railway, Alresford
- Farnborough Air Sciences Museum
- Sammy Miller Motorcycle Museum, New Milton
- Romsey Signal Box
- Farnborough Centrifuge (original 1950s centrifuge to research G-force on pilots)
- Calshot Castle (including exhibits of Calshot seaplanes)

4

JOURNEYS

ADVENTURERS

St Boniface, also known as Winfrid, was a monk at Nursling Monastery. He sailed to Germany in 716 CE and for the last thirty-six years of his life was a missionary converting the pagans in Germany to Christianity. He also reformed the Frankish Church and made friends with the Pope. It has been written that no Englishman has had a greater influence on European history than Boniface. That's certainly some legacy! He also wrote some riddles, a favourite Anglo-Saxon pastime, and a grammar book, *Ars grammatica* (no giggling!), among other works.

For some, Hampshire was the last English place they would see before going to unknown lands. Following two frankly disastrous attempts to begin a British settlement in America in Virginia in 1587 and 1607, a further venture to found a colony in Virginia began in 1610 in which a Thomas West, Lord de la Warr, native of Wherwell, played a large part. A charter was obtained from King James I in 1610 and West was appointed sole governor of the colony, avoiding the catastrophic disputes between the councillors that had plagued the 1607 attempt. He arrived at the James River in 1610 and persuaded the previous colonists to stay as they had been about to abandon the place altogether. He restored order, introduced reforms that allowed men to take leases of land, established tobacco as a crop, constructed forts and founded the new town of Hampton. He returned home to England, ill, in 1611 but his deputy, Sir Thomas Dale, carried on the reforms and the numbers of settlers rose to 350. Lord de la Warr's practical and strong intervention saved the colony from extinction and gave him a place in America's history. He is remembered not only through the successful colony, which became the state of Virginia, but also through the Delaware River and the US state named after him.

In August 1620 two ships were due to set sail from Southampton, the *Mayflower* and the *Speedwell*, destined for America and a new life free from religious persecution. The Separatists, who wanted a new life free from the Church of England, had rendezvoused at Southampton from London and Holland. There they slept in their ships moored at West Quay and bought supplies and gained advice for their voyage. To the 102 Pilgrims and thirty crew, they also added one more family: that of Stephen Hopkins. He had experience of America, having been wrecked on Bermuda in 1609 and then subsequently living in Jamestown.

On 15 August the two ships set sail, but they weren't to know that before they could get into the open ocean, they would have to stop twice because of leaks in the *Speedwell* and in the end continue from Plymouth in the *Mayflower*, one ship down. Hopkins's wife gave birth to another child on board, who was named Oceanus. Hopkins became one of the foremost men of the settlement, making contact with the Native Americans. They set up a settlement in modern Massachusetts, at Plymouth, negotiating with the Wampanoag tribe, who helped them survive. After a difficult winter, fifty-three surviving colonists remained and for their harvest of 1621 they held a three-day festival of prayer, known as the first Thanksgiving. The first National Day of Mourning was held in 1970, on the same day, to acknowledge the devastation the landing of the Pilgrims wrought on the native people of Massachusetts.

Lord Carnarvon, the discoverer of the tomb of Tutankhamun in 1922 with Howard Carter, is buried at the top of Beacon Hill overlooking Highclere Castle, his family seat. Beacon Hill is the home of another ancient site, albeit a tad colder: an Iron Age fort. You can see the plaque and the fenced grave where it describes him as 'Adventurer, Explorer, Archaeologist'.

The transportation fleets for the penal colony at Port Jackson, Sydney Cove, Australia, departed from Portsmouth. Although perhaps seeming a less weighty sentence than execution, in practice the journey was extremely hazardous. This was particularly so for the second fleet, leaving Portsmouth in January 1790, with just over 1,000 convicts in three ships, including twenty-seven Hampshire people. The conditions were truly appalling, similar to slave ships, with no exercise or fresh air and paltry water and food rations. A total of 267 died on the voyage, while 486 landed sick with 124 of those dying soon after they arrived, mainly from scurvy, dysentery, fever or starvation.

Those prisoners from Hampshire that did survive were among the pioneers of the first Australian settlements and included such characters as John Bagley and Thomas Phillips. They had been sentenced for stealing various items from Henry Winscomb of Winchester and a shirt from Martin Filer of Winchester, and both were free by 1802 and holding land at Mulgrave Place, 30 miles from Sydney. Another, John Hunt, was free by 1802 and working as a 'shingle-splitter' in Parramatta. Charles George was also free and working as a servant at Kissing Point in 1828, 10 miles west of Sydney. Charles Smith was sentenced for stealing hay and was a gardener in Sydney by 1814. Samuel Howell had stolen clothes at Wallop and was sentenced to transportation for life, but is found in a census as a blacksmith working in Sydney in 1814.

CONQUERING THE ICE FROM HAMPSHIRE

George Marston, born on Addison Road, Southsea in 1882, was the expedition artist with Ernest Shackleton on two of his trips to the Antarctic in the golden age of polar exploration. On the first one he was one of the team members to publish

'*At the edge of the crater*', *an etching by George Marston from* Aurora Australis, *the first book published on the continent of Antarctica. It shows the party who climbed to the top of Mount Erebus.*

the first book, *Aurora Australis,* in 1908, entirely produced on the continent of Antarctica. It was written, illustrated, printed and bound there (using packing case boards) under extremely difficult circumstances. Only 75 to 100 copies were made. He was also on the famous *Endurance* expedition of 1914–16, in which Shackleton and his team all got home safely despite incredible hardships and dangers, after being trapped in the ice. Marston was an extremely practical, fit, cheerful and creative team member and was to the fore in all the dramatic parts of the horrifying adventure. His oil paints were used to waterproof the seams of the open boats they needed to sail to Elephant Island after the *Endurance* was crushed by ice, and he masterminded the crew's shelter on Elephant Island, made of their upturned boats.

Another Antarctic explorer with a more tangential connection to Hampshire was Captain Scott. He was sent, at the age of 12, to Stubbington House, in Fareham, to complete an education that would see him become a Navy Cadet.

On Scott's first Antarctic expedition as commander, on board the *Discovery* was William Lashley, born and raised in Hambledon, son of a thatcher. He was considered a fit, healthy and reliable team member and he undertook an exploratory trip to Victoria Land in 1903. Amid fears the *Discovery* would get stuck in the Antarctic ice, the expedition returned and docked at Stokes Bay in autumn 1904. She was then escorted into Portsmouth Harbour with a guard of honour from all the naval ships.

Lashley returned to Antarctica with Scott in the 1911–13 *Terra Nova* expedition. His incredible strength was shown on the return journey, the party having gone most of the way to the pole. He and Crean pulled their fellow teammate, Evans, who had collapsed from scurvy, most of the way by sledge. Lashley then stayed to nurse him while Crean completed the 35 miles needed to base camp. Lashley returned to Hambledon in 1932 and built his house there, called Minna Bluff, on East Street.

George Mallory, naturally adventurous and with a head for heights, even as a small boy, attended Winchester College on a mathematics scholarship in 1909. Here he learnt to climb with a master, George Irving. Irving was a controversial figure who had a big impact on Mallory's climbing, in a club they called the Winchester Ice Club. Mallory famously free-climbed the college chapel tower. He went on to lead three expeditions to climb Everest, the last in 1924 taking his life (and his partner Irvine's) and in which he may or may not have reached the summit. His biographer, David Pye, gives us an insight into his personality: 'There is no doubt that all his life he enjoyed taking risks, or perhaps it would be fairer to say doing things with a small margin of safety. He always caught a train by five seconds rather than five minutes: a trait annoying to his companions, and not less so because he always justified it by not missing the train.'

His memorial, which hangs in the cloister of Winchester College, is a stone worked in opus sectile by Reginald 'Dick' Gleadowe, who also attended Winchester College and returned there in 1923 as its drawing master. It shows Mallory climbing, beautifully depicted in marble and limestone interlocking pieces, and it tells us he was 'lost to human sight between Heaven and Earth' around 800ft from the summit of Everest.

Guy Bullock also attended Winchester College and was a member of the Winchester Ice Club with Mallory. He was an experienced climber and went on the 1921 expedition to Everest. He discovered with Mallory a route to the North Col of Everest via the Lhakpa La Col, paving the way for future attempts of the summit.

ROYAL JOURNEYS

On 1 February 1901, *Alberta*, carrying the coffin of Queen Victoria, slowly steamed from Cowes, Isle of Wight, across the Spithead anchorage. She was accompanied by the mournful firing of guns from both Royal Navy and foreign ships, and then the Gosport and Portsmouth fortification guns. She berthed at Gosport and the next morning Victoria's body was taken to Windsor for her funeral.

King Charles I was held prisoner in Carisbrooke Castle on the Isle of Wight after he lost the Civil War. He was transferred to Hurst Castle on the Hampshire mainland for nineteen days in December 1648, but then began his journey to London to begin his trial and ultimately his execution. His journey took him via Winchester, where he was met at the Westgate by a city delegation including the mayor. As the (Royalist) mayor moved to make a speech and welcome the king to the city he was threatened violently and the king was moved on, ever closer to his death on 30 January 1649.

King William II (or William Rufus) was killed accidentally while out hunting in the New Forest in 1100. It may not have been an accident, we'll never know, but we do know his companions and his brother left him rather indecently and it was left to a charcoal burner called Purkis to transport him to Winchester for burial. He lugged the king onto his two-wheeled cart and took him 25 miles to the royal city; 'blood dripped from the body all the way,' according to William of Malmesbury. The route is disputed but Bell Street in Romsey is said to be one way he took, as is Red Lane in Compton and Kings Road in Chandler's Ford.

On Wednesday 19 July 1554, around 2 p.m., Prince Philip of Spain and his fleet arrived in Southampton for his forthcoming nuptials to Mary Tudor in Winchester. He stayed in the royal apartments at Southampton castle and 400 servants were lodged in Southampton, apparently having a royal stag do from Thursday until Sunday. On Monday, Philip left Southampton in heavy rain, accompanied by a great guard of English archers, crossbowmen and halberdiers, 3,000 horses and 'a great many servants richly adorned'. By the time they neared Winchester the rain had made Philip pretty unpresentable to meet his bride, so he stopped at St Cross Hospital and changed into a black velvet surcoat covered with gold bugles and a suit of white velvet trimmed in the same way. The mud-spattered horses were replaced with horses that Mary sent. He was greeted at Southgate with a racket of trumpets, bells and cannon shots. The mayor and bailiffs, in their red robes, knelt down to present the keys of the city and castle to Philip. He accepted them, but immediately handed them back. The procession then rode through the city, Philip visited the cathedral, then went to his lodgings in the Deanery. That evening he met Mary for the first time in the bishop's garden before marrying her the next day.

The Monarch's Way long-distance path is based on the long six-week route taken by 21-year-old not-yet-King Charles II, after his defeat by Cromwell in the final battle of the Civil War at Worcester in 1651. He started in Worcester and 625 miles later finally escaped from Shoreham. His route in Hampshire was via Houghton, King's Somborne, Old Winchester Hill, Hambledon and Horndean.

GATEWAY TO THE EMPIRE

The great transatlantic steam liners of the 1900s were based at Southampton. The great steamship companies began with the Royal Mail Steam Packet Co. in 1842, then the Union Line sailing to South Africa in 1857, then the transatlantic American Line came to Southampton in 1893. In 1907, the White Star line transferred its operations to the city's docks, as did Cunard in 1919, making it the largest passenger terminal in the country. Between the wars it became 'the gateway to the Empire' and in 1938, for example, it saw 560,000 ocean-going passengers, along with 18.5 million tons of shipping and 2,500 trains. It is still a passenger hub today: 2019 saw 1.8 million cruise passengers from 520 calling passenger ships. Each one is estimated to give £1.25 million to the local economy. P&O, Celebrity, Princess, Royal Caribbean and Cunard still use Southampton as their base.

Luxury liners weren't the only way to tour the world from Southampton between the wars; the long, straight and calm stretch of Southampton Water was also the scene of glamorous Imperial Airways' flying boats. They arrived from and left for all corners of the Empire, as it was then, docking at the Marine Air Terminal (where the decaying pontoons can be seen today). In the 1930s flying boats were used instead of land planes on the major route through the British Empire, where there were more waterways than runways. Southampton Water saw departures to South Africa via the Mediterranean, Nile and East Africa, and to Australia via the Far East and India. The first all-air service began between Southampton and Alexandria in 1937 with low-altitude, height-of-luxury aircraft including saloon bars, restaurants and private cabins. India could be reached within three days of England and South Africa took five days. A Short Sandringham seaplane that is representative of the air fleet and a reconstructed plane cocktail bar are on display at the Solent Sky Museum.

PUSHING THE ENVELOPE

Alec Rose circumnavigated the globe single-handedly in his yacht, the *Lively Lady*, in 1968. He was Hampshire-grown, owning a greengrocer's shop in Southsea which his daughter ran while he was away. His journey was followed very closely by the public and he arrived back at Southsea on 4 July 1968, just before his sixtieth birthday, cheered by thousands of people on the seafront. He opened the Bamboo House Chinese restaurant in Southsea in 1968. *Lively Lady* is now on display at Portsmouth Historic Dockyard.

Dickie Frost was an incredible all-round athlete but excelled especially in cycling. At the peak of his racing career in 1898 he won the country's two leading cycle racing trophies and the National Cycling Championship in just one fortnight. He devoted his later life to fostering a love of sport in Hampshire youngsters. He lived his whole life at No. 15 The Square, Winchester, where he ran a jewellery business.

Zara Rutherford was a student at St Swithun's School in Winchester and took a rather unusual gap-year project in 2022 – she completed a solo flight around the world, the youngest person to do so at age 19. She used a Shark Ultralight, the world's fastest light aircraft, with the spare seat removed to make room for an extra fuel tank.

In 1895, Evelyn Ellis wanted to deliberately break the law that said all road vehicles had to have a man waving a red flag in front of them, thereby limiting their speed to 4mph. His aim was to show the absurdity of it. He had a Panhard-Levassor car made for him in France with a Daimler engine and shipped over to Southampton Docks. Mindful that policemen could be lurking at Southampton Docks and even Winchester and Eastleigh stations, he arranged for the car to be carried from the docks by rail to Micheldever, the first out-of-the-way, small railway station. Here, on 5 July 1895, he began his journey to his home at Datchet, with engineer Frederick Simms. Simms noted:

> We set forth at exactly 9.26 am and made good progress on the well-made London coaching road … It was a very pleasing sensation to go along the delightful roads towards Virginia Water at speeds varying from three to twenty miles per hour, and our iron horse performed splendidly. There we took our luncheon and fed our engine with a little oil. Going down the steep hill leading to Windsor we passed through Datchet and arrived in front of the entrance hall of Mr Ellis's house at Datchet at 5.40 pm, thus completing our most enjoyable journey of 56 miles, the first ever made by a petroleum motor carriage in this country in 5 hours and 32 minutes, exclusive of stoppages and at an average speed of 9.84 mph.

It worked and the law was repealed in 1896.

5

DISASTERS

Life hasn't always run smoothly in Hampshire. Here are some of the more disastrous events in its history, although some have a silver lining.

LIFE AND DEATH IN TUDOR HAMPSHIRE

The sinking of the *Mary Rose* on 19 July 1545 was a disaster for King Henry VIII but a great opportunity for archaeologists of the twentieth century, who were able to learn so much about Tudor life from the well-preserved items under the silt of the Solent. She was the pride of Henry VIII's greatly expanded fleet and was engaged in action against the King of France's fleet intent on invading England. She sank quickly, perhaps because she dipped her heavily loaded gunports too low below the water. Humiliating, disappointing and deeply saddening, Henry watched her go down from Southsea Castle.

The *Mary Rose* in numbers:

Built: 1510
Sank: 1545
For King Henry: 8
Faced French fleet of: 225 ships

Drowned on board: around 500 (200 mariners, 185 soldiers, 30 gunners and the officers)

Survived: 35

Number of guns when sank: 91

Salvage attempts in: 1545, 1836 and 1978–82

Located on seabed (again): 1978

Number of volunteer divers used (1978–82): 500

Number of diving hours during excavations: 23,000

Number of objects recovered: 19,000

Number of nit combs recovered: 80 (some with nits on)

Number of linstocks (wooden 'arms' for lighting guns) recovered: 44

Number of shoes found: over 400

Number of woodworking planes recovered: 22

Number of gold 'angels' (or coins with St Michael on) found: 29

Number of dog bodies recovered: 1

Number of human bodies recovered: 179

Number of rat bodies recovered: 3 (apparently they are good swimmers!)

Raised in: 1982

Turned upright: 1985

Number of years sprayed with cold water (after raising her): 12

Number of years of polyethylene glycol solution spraying (after the water spraying): 19

Number of years drying out using the 'hot-box chamber' method: 3

Tons of water removed during drying: 100

Date anchor was found and raised: 2005

New museum opened: 2013

Ship revealed for first time conserved and dried: 2016

WINCHESTER'S WEAK WINCH

King Alfred might seem like he rules the world standing at the end of the Broadway in Winchester, but the installation of the 5.2m statue in 1901 was far from straightforward. Once the massive Cornish granite plinth had been brought from the station on a steam engine and installed and the statue had been cast by Hamo Thorneycroft, the job of getting it on top of the plinth began. While winching it up, two men were seriously injured when the poles of the winch gave way, so the opening had to be delayed six weeks. Further, when moving the two stones and the statue into position on top of the plinth, granules of sugar had apparently been used as a 'lubricant'. This, however, subsequently melted in the hot weather and, dripping down the plinth, it looked like blood – not the look the city organisers were looking for – and it began to attract wasps! The fire brigade had to use their hoses to spray away the sugar. Finally, a grand opening ceremony took place, although I hope nobody told them they got the date wrong – Mayor Alfred Bowker had worked the project to celebrate 1,000 years since King Alfred's death, but he mistakenly thought it was 901, and we now know it was 899 – whoops!

EXCRUCIATING EXCOMMUNICATION

Excommunication and indictment by the Pope were seriously bad news in pre-Reformation England. If implemented it meant no baptisms (with consecrated oil), marriages or funeral services or burials in consecrated land could be carried out; there was a serious risk of going to hell for the king's subjects; and the throne was vulnerable to Church-backed usurping. King John so upset the Pope in 1209 that he was indicted and excommunicated. By 1213 he had to negotiate his way back into the Pope's good books and this happened in Winchester. The Archbishop of Canterbury and other bishops couldn't enter the cathedral due to the excommunication so they met in the Chapter House in the Cathedral Close. Here John promised to maintain the ancient laws of England and was absolved.

The pillars at the entrance to the Chapter House, Winchester Cathedral, the site of King John's absolution on 20 July 1213.

In 1450 the inhabitants of Portsmouth were excommunicated as a result of their murder of the Bishop of Chichester, Adam Moleyns, at the Domus Dei church (now the Garrison Church) in Portsmouth. He had been sent to make a reduced payment to the shipmen of Portsmouth because of their unruly behaviour during church services. Unruly behaviour led to docking pay, docking pay led to murder, murder led to excommunication. The church was eventually rebuilt and the excommunication lifted after fifty years.

WOOLSTON'S WOEFUL WORKS

Supermarine's iconic Spitfire hardly needs an introduction and played a huge role in the winning of the Second World War. However, it nearly didn't get off the ground, as it were, despite successful test flights. The Spitfire's maiden flight, at Southampton Airport on 5 March 1936, confirmed its awesome potential: 'It really looked as if we were going to have something that could match up to anything the Germans could build,' recalled Group Captain Frederick Winterbotham. However, the type of fighter-to-fighter air combat that ensued in the war was not envisaged and the RAF seemed to see the Spitfire initially as an inferior fighter plane.

The Supermarine works at Woolston was also short on facilities, space and staff and had never undertaken orders on any scale, so building Spitfires between 1936 and 1939 was plagued with mismanagement and technical difficulties. The Secretary of State for Air described Supermarine's approach as 'totally unacceptable'. They subcontracted out and extended their Woolston factory, and eventually production was brought under control and the Spitfire became the icon of the RAF it is today – but it nearly didn't happen.

The Woolston Spitfire factory was destroyed by two daylight bombing raids in September 1940, killing 110 people. However, the works simply moved out to whatever premises they could find in Southampton and all through Hampshire including laundries, bus stations and the grand Hursley House – where hangars were put up in stable yards, the linen room was turned into a laboratory, the wine cellar became a dark room and the ballroom was the drawing office.

WINCHESTER'S WONKY WALLS

Winchester Cathedral has a rather squat tower, especially compared to the soaring spire of its neighbouring cathedral at Salisbury. This may be because it is the second tower, the first having completely fallen down in 1107, nearly taking the whole cathedral with it. The Norman cathedral was built between 1079 and 1093, a mere fifteen years. Shortcuts were presumably taken, resulting in some wobbly parts of the structure. You can still see pillars leaning very out of true in the North Transept. The tower couldn't even withstand fifteen years before it fell. Some superstitious types think it may be because the 'bad' king William Rufus was buried under the tower in 1100.

EXPENSIVE AND UNUSED

In 1418 the *Grace Dieu* was commissioned by King Henry V and built by William Soper at Southampton. It was the largest ship ever built in England at that time, weighing over 1,400 tons, using perhaps 3,700 trees and 23 tons of iron. It was never used for war and ended up moored on the River Hamble, where it was struck by lightning in 1439 and sank. It still lies there; a yellow marker marks the spot of the wreck.

Not all Hampshire's aviation experiments got off the ground (or water). In 1914 Luke & Co., an amalgamation of a yacht-building firm and a motorboat business, attempted to build a large seaplane at Hamble. The HL1 was a two-seat, single-engine biplane with two floats (to land on) and a 60ft wing span. It dominated the 1914 Olympia Aero Show (although unfinished) but later proved unsuccessful. As the plane's floats and body were constructed more like yacht hulls, it could barely get off the water. It was also supplied with its own seaplane clinker dinghy!

In December 1945, Saunders-Roe began work on a giant flying boat for the UK–New York route. An absolutely huge beast, with ten turbine-propeller engines, it could take 100 passengers 5,000 miles at a speed of 370mph. The name Princess was chosen, although it doesn't quite fit the lumbering, heavy-bellied hulls of the planes. The price went up from £2.8 million to £10 million. One Princess was launched in 1952, 'running high and proud in the Solent like an ocean liner with wings', but the others lay unfinished and all three were cocooned at Calshot and eventually scrapped.

DISASTROUS OYSTERS

The Great Oyster Scare of 1902 at Emsworth rather finished off this local industry. Emsworth supplied thousands of oysters throughout the country, but in 1902 guests at a banquet in Winchester became ill and the Dean of Winchester died from typhoid after eating Emsworth oysters. The oyster beds were found to be contaminated badly with sewage. Sales plummeted and ended the livelihood of many virtually overnight.

A STRING OF WHITE STAR LINE DISASTERS

On 20 September 1911, the White Star liner *Olympic* left Southampton for New York. It was the largest passenger liner in the world at 45,230 tons. As it was coming out of Southampton Water, a navy vessel, HMS *Hawke,* came alongside it, but then took a sharp turn to port and rammed the *Olympic* near its stern with a huge noise and left a massive triangular hole. The *Olympic* anchored in Osborne Bay on the Isle of Wight while all passengers were taken off in tenders. Incredibly there was no loss of life. It appears most of the passengers were having lunch rather than in their cabins.

Olympic made the journey back to Belfast, where it was completely overhauled. To save time it was refitted with a propeller from its sister ship, then being built in the Belfast dock too, *Titanic*. This delayed *Titanic*'s departure from Southampton by one month. And that gives us a tantalising 'what if …?' moment.

Captain Smith was the captain of *Olympic* on 20 September, and George Bowyer was the pilot that helped them out of Southampton Water. Smith in command and Bowyer as pilot were also in place on 10 April 1912 as the White Star's newest ship left Southampton – *Titanic*. There was a near miss in the first few minutes of the voyage again, when *Titanic* nearly hit the American liner *New York*. But, clearly, worse was to come.

What seemed to be a boon to Southampton when *Titanic* was fitted out, crewed and supplied in the city before its maiden voyage, turned into a great disaster for the city when the ship was lost on 15 April 1912. Supply contracts had gone to local firms for fresh fruit and vegetables, and even Bealings nursery to provide 400 plants for the ship plus buttonhole flowers for each first-class passenger, and of course many of the crew were recruited from the city and Hampshire as a whole. Many had joined the ship to find work after the national coal strike of 1912, which had left many starving and relying on handouts. The city of Southampton gave 724 members of *Titanic* crew and only 175 returned. Hampshire gave an additional fifty-four crew, of which fifteen survived. A total of 1,517 drowned on *Titanic*. As news filtered through, crew and passengers' family members gathered outside Canute Chambers, the offices of the White Star Line.

The areas of Northam, Chapel and St Mary's were particularly hard hit. In one school in Northam, 120 children out of 250 had lost a father. The RMS Titanic Relief Fund was set up by public subscription to give help to dependents of lost crew. Charity events were arranged and even charity records were sold in aid of the fund – gramophone, of course. The city still remembers the terrible disaster for local families. As well as the Sea City Museum, there are memorials: for the Engineers in Andrews Park; the Titanic Musicians Memorial in Cumberland Place; a plaque to Millvina Dean in the Memorial Garden near Sea City Museum, the youngest to be rescued and the last living survivor; a plaque to the postal workers who died and a Book of Remembrance in the Civic Centre; two commemorative oak plaques of Northam parish to commemorate their dead, now in Sea City Museum; two plaques at Holy Trinity Church at Millbrook; a crew memorial in Holyrood Church and a memorial window in St Mary's Church depicting 685 bubbles of water, one for every member of the crew that died.

STRANGE SHIPWRECKS

A terrible catastrophe happened at Spithead on 29 August 1782 while a ship was at anchor! It had a huge impact throughout England due to the loss of life and the trauma it elicited. The massive 100-gun *Royal George* was at Spithead undergoing repairs. Everything happened very quickly: suddenly it was flooded with water, there was a huge, heavy crack and the ship capsized and sank in minutes. It was thought that when it was listing to port to undertake repairs, it listed too far and water came in the lower gun ports. This was combined with rotten timbers and led them to give way. In only 90ft of water, the mast and bowsprit could still be seen by the many people who flocked to the wreck. Over 900 men and women died, it is believed – but due to the fact it was taking on supplies and many traders would have been on board, the death toll may well have been higher.

The sinking of Royal George. *An illustration of the event from the novel* Poor Jack *by Captain Maryatt.*

The incredible story of HMS *Pique* is told by the inscription above a huge stone at Portsmouth Historic Dockyard (at the end of the Porter's Garden on College Road), where it limped home from the Labrador coast:

This stone was found wedged in a hole in the bottom of the
Frigate H.M.S. PIQUE, (c/o Captain the
Hon. H.J. Rous, R.N.) when the
ship was docked in Portsmouth in October 1835. The PIQUE,
had run ashore in the Belle Isle Straits, Labrador, in Sept.
of that year. After refloating herself, she sailed across the
Atlantic, without a rudder & with pumps continuously manned
to control her leaks. But for this stone acting as a plug to one
of the larger Holes, she would, certainly have foundered.
A splendid feat of seamanship.

Apparently a further leak was stopped by a swollen sack of ship's biscuits!

The Navy's submarine service is based in Gosport, Hampshire, and so is its museum. The first naval submarine was called *Holland 1* and is in the museum. There are several wrecks of submarines in the Solent, including *A-1*, which collided with the steamer *Berwick Castle* while on exercise in 1904. It was recovered and repaired but suffered an explosion in 1910. *A-4* sank in 1905 to 90ft, but due to its commander's cool actions it resurfaced again four minutes later. As it was towed into Portsmouth Harbour, it suffered two huge explosions and sank beneath the waves.

Even a hovercraft has suffered injury – but only once, on 4 March 1972. Hovertravel's SR-N6 012 was en route from Ryde to Southsea with twenty-six people on board, it was about a quarter of a mile off Southsea when it was hit by an unusually large wave, causing the vehicle to capsize with the loss of five lives.

THE GREAT SURVIVOR

It seems you couldn't destroy *Victory* even if you wanted to. She survived attacking the French at Toulon in 1793, the Battle of Cape Vincent in 1797, being fitted out as a hospital ship, then refitted – known as 'The Great Repair' – and sent back into service, then the Battle of Trafalgar in 1805, being rammed by HMS *Neptune* in 1903 while afloat in Portsmouth Harbour and the Blitz, which virtually flattened the rest of Portsmouth. Now in dry dock in Portsmouth, she still needs continuing conservation to save her from the ravages of time.

RUN AGROUND

On 12 January 1934, HMS *Nelson* ran aground in Portsmouth Harbour. She was stuck fast most of the day and efforts to move her off the mud included the ship's company dancing up and down on deck to music and five destroyers ordered to circle her at speed – this did the job apparently and their wake floated her free.

AND ONE INLAND WRECK ...

William Walker, a diver, worked on a rather different Hampshire 'wreck'. After Navy training at the Diving School HMS *Excellent* in Portsmouth, he became Chief Diver for Siebe, Gorman & Co. and worked on their experiments on the physiological effects of pressure. In 1906 he was called to work in Hampshire again, to Winchester Cathedral. At the time the huge church was described as a sinking ship, nearly ready to break its back! The east end had been built on an old riverbed, a mixture of clays and peat and water, and it was now sinking into that ground at an alarming angle, with several huge cracks in its walls. A massive restoration project was needed, but they needed a diver to go under the walls, into trenches now filled with water, and lay good foundations. Walker was hired and managed to do the work over six years (with a team of workmen working once the water source was stemmed by Walker's work and pumped away), saving the ancient cathedral from collapse.

AIR ACCIDENTS

Samuel Kinkead was a First World War fighter ace; member of the Schneider Trophy 1927 team; record breaker (he registered the fastest speed of a biplane seaplane of the time at 277.18mph) and known as one of the best high-speed fighter pilots in the RAF, adept at landing on sea. Which makes it all the more mysterious when he died in 1928 near Calshot, after his plane plunged into the sea attempting to be the first pilot to fly at over 5 miles per minute, and witnessed by a crowd of onlookers. He was buried in Fawley graveyard with full military honours and it took four RAF lorries to bring all the floral tributes to his funeral. The inquest found it was pilot error, but there remains a mystery surrounding his death as he was such a virtuoso pilot.

The *Lebaudy Morning Post* was a French-made semi-rigid airship built for the British Army. It flew across the Channel in 1911 and made it safely to Hampshire. It maintained a rip in its envelope (the balloon part) on delivery to the airship hangar at Farnborough Balloon Factory but was soon repaired. However, its next flight was to prove its last. On landing, the ropes could not be held and it ran into some trees, bursting the envelope and destroying it over the trees and Woodlands Cottage, home of Lady Mildred Follett. Rather an expensive disaster.

Farnborough Air Show is held in even years and is one of the most important of its type in the world, showcasing some of the newest technology in aviation. It has had its fair share of airborne accidents, the worst in 1952 when a De Havilland Sea Vixen crashed into the crowd, killing thirty-one people including its crew. It led to more stringent safety restrictions at air shows.

BAD YEARS IN HAMPSHIRE

The following years were bad years to be in Hampshire, to be avoided if possible:

- 1141 – the Anarchy civil war came to Winchester. King Stephen's forces (under his Queen Matilda and his brother Bishop Henri de Blois) and Empress Matilda's forces fought it out in the Rout of Winchester, burning the city between them in the process.

- 1642 – another Civil War, this time between Parliamentarians and Royalists. The Parliamentarians took Winchester in this year and proceeded to plunder and destroy the cathedral and its priceless books and archives, throwing some into the river and destroying the stained-glass windows. Worse was to come in 1644 when the castle was also taken.

- 1349 – the Black Death came to Hampshire. Southampton is thought to perhaps be the place where it entered England, according to contemporary writer Henry Knighton. The first deaths were recorded in Titchfield in October 1348 and it was at its worst in spring 1349. Nearly 50 per cent of Winchester clergy died, including the Prior of St Swithun's and the Abbess of Romsey. Southampton's population reduced from around 2,500 to around 1,600 in 1377. In Winchester the estimated population drop was from around 10,000 to 3,000–5,000 in 1377.

- 1338 – Southampton and Portsmouth were destroyed by French raiders at the beginning of the Hundred Years' War, exposing their defences as woefully inadequate. There was much burning, massacre and even slave-taking.

- 1536–39 – Hampshire's thirteen monasteries were closed and their assets taken by the crown. Together 261 people lost their homes and a quarter of Hampshire manors went to the crown. The schools, hospitals and almshouses they ran disappeared and their artworks were 'redistributed'.

- 1912 – over 1,000 Southampton families and many Hampshire people were affected by the death toll of *Titanic*.

• 1940 – The south coast cities of Southampton and Portsmouth suffered badly in the Blitz, being targeted by German bombers because of their docks and aeroplane manufacturing sites (often using Ordnance Survey maps made in Southampton!). Over 630 people in Southampton died from German bombing raids and 930 people were killed in Portsmouth over four years, with 6,000 Portsmouth homes destroyed and around 75,000 suffering some bomb damage.

6

CREATIVE HAMPSHIRE

THREE BOHEMIAN ARTISTS IN HAMPSHIRE

Flora Twort
Flora attended The Slade to train as an artist, but also had a strong practical streak and she opened a bookshop in Petersfield with two friends. This became a hotspot for artist and writer friends and her paintings of Petersfield are an insight into life in a gentler time. See her work at the Flora Twort Gallery in Petersfield.

Augustus John
John was the foremost portrait painter of the 1920s. He moved to Fryern Court, Fordingbridge, in 1927 and lived there until his death in 1961. He was known for living a 'bohemian' lifestyle at Fryern Court, which became an open house for many artists including T.E. Shaw and Dylan Thomas. He was a great advocate of gypsies' rights and owned a vardo, or gypsy wagon, himself. He was known among the New Forest gypsies as their king and they called him Sir Gustus. He is buried in Stuckton Road cemetery and there is a statue of him in Fordingbridge, near the bridge.

Dora Carrington

An underrated artist, known more for her unorthodox lifestyle and who was associated with the Bloomsbury Group. After graduating from the Slade School of Art, in 1914 she moved to her parents' house, Ibthorpe House, in Hurstbourne Tarrant and set up a studio. You can see a rare piece of hers at Portsmouth Museum and Art Gallery: a large gramophone painted with her images.

TWO HAMPSHIRE SHEPHERDS AND MASTERS

Heywood Sumner was an important figure of the Arts and Crafts movement and son of Mary Sumner, founder of the Mothers' Union. His early life was in No. 1 The Close, Winchester, with his parents and he later moved to Gorley in the New Forest. He produced Sgraffito decoration in churches, etchings, illustrations and wallpaper designs. He also illustrated J.R. Wise's *The New Forest* and published Hampshire folk songs in *The Besom Maker and other Country Folk Songs*. He was one of the early

The fairy ring pound in Pinnick, by Heywood Sumner.

Masters of the Art Workers' Guild, an organisation based in Bloomsbury that sought to bring together the fine and applied arts on an equal footing, and his fellow members took to calling him 'The Shepherd' when he regaled them with Hampshire folk songs! But in 1904, in his mid-40s, he moved to Gorley and took up archaeology. He excavated many sites, often single-handedly, and studied the landscape, geology and folklore of the New Forest.

Tracey Sheppard is a Winchester-based, but nationally renowned, glass engraver and was also Master of the Art Workers Guild in 2022. Her beautiful work can be seen in the Epiphany Chapel of Winchester Cathedral; the entrance of St Lawrence, the Square, Winchester; in Hyde Abbey Gardens, Winchester; and churches at Boldre, Hurstbourne Tarrant, Wickham and Romsey Abbey.

WALL PAINTINGS

Rex Whistler painted the wonderful trompe l'oeil on every wall of the saloon at Mottisfont House (now a National Trust site) while he was staying with Gilbert and Maud Russell in 1939. Maud commissioned Rex to complete the murals to reflect the house's thirteenth-century history and it looks like a medieval Gothic-vaulted room with plaster mouldings and sumptuous curtains – the incredible 3D realism all created with paint.

Stanley Spencer was commissioned to paint the interior of the Sandham Memorial Chapel, in Burghclere, in 1927. His patrons, Mr and Mrs John Behrend, commissioned the chapel as a memorial to Lieutenant H.W. Sandham, Mary Behrend's brother, who was killed in the First World War. Completed in 1932 and now owned by the National Trust, it is one of the most impressive, poignant and original artworks to be born from the First World War.

The Holy Sepulchre Chapel in Winchester Cathedral has some of the oldest and best-preserved wall paintings in the country. It can be found off the North Aisle and is open around Easter but can be viewed from outside the rest of the time. The walls were painted in the twelfth and thirteenth centuries and were hidden from view for centuries with later paintings on top of them, hence the preservation. They depict Christ being taken down from the cross and his entombment in incredible colour. They are complemented by an altar cloth by Alice Kettle, contemporary textile artist, of the same subject and colours.

A little further east in the cathedral is the Guardian Angels chapel dating from the 1200s. Its ceiling features angels peering down through portals from heaven, represented by swirls and stars. It was painted by Master William, the king's painter, and even though it was painted three centuries after the heyday of the Winchester School of art, elements of its style can still be seen in the angels.

There are six large-scale murals all over the Hampshire coast and Isle of Wight depicting strange and wonderful creatures of the Solent. Commissioned as part of the Hampshire and Isle of Wight Wildlife Trust's Secrets of the Solent project and painted by street artist ATM, spot them in prominent places if you can. They include a spider crab, thresher shark, a seahorse, harbour seal and cuttlefish.

A wall painting dating from the late ninth century, right at the time of King Alfred, was found in the excavations of New Minster, the Saxon monastery in Winchester. It is almost a unique survival of Anglo-Saxon painted decoration and the wide-eyed figure was probably one of several depicted in a heavenly choir. See it at the Winchester Cathedral exhibition, Kings and Scribes.

STORIES IN STITCH

Hampshire has a rich heritage of stitch craft, through which it can tell many of its stories.

D-Day is recreated in visual form by the Overlord Embroidery, housed where many troops left for the beaches of Normandy – Southsea – in the D-Day Story Museum. Thirty-four panels (83m) of hand-stitched embroidery tell the story from preparations to battle to legacy. It was designed by Sandra Lawrence and stitched by embroiderers from the Royal School of Needlework. Thirty-four preparatory painted panels now hang in the Pentagon, in Washington DC.

In a twist of history, it is also thought that the *Overlord Embroidery's* inspiration, the *Bayeaux Tapestry*, telling the story of a previous invasion, may also have been stitched in Hampshire. One of the contenders for the English embroiderers of the Norman invasion story are the nuns of St Mary's Abbey in Winchester, who were renowned in the eleventh century for their skill with needle and thread.

The oldest example of medieval embroidery in the world is displayed in Durham Cathedral but was worked in St Mary's Abbey, also known as Nunnaminster, in Winchester. The Maniple and Stole of St Cuthbert were found in his coffin when it was opened in 1827. They were probably given to the northern church by King Athelstan. They are worked in coloured silks and gold thread.

Heywood Sumner, the Arts and Craft artist who lived in the New Forest, designed a tapestry in 1908 called *The Chace*. It depicts a hunt of a deer in the New Forest with two magnificent beech trees and hounds. It is now a treasure of the Hampshire Cultural Trust Collections.

Another New Forest-inspired embroidery hangs in the New Forest Heritage Centre in Lyndhurst. *The New Forest Embroidery* celebrates the 900th anniversary of the forest and depicts nature, people and places. It was designed by Belinda, Lady Montagu, with over sixty volunteer embroiderers' help.

Looking Forwards to the Past is an epic piece of embroidery (16.5m by 3m) by Alice Kettle, international textile artist and Winchester native, and is on display at The Arc, Winchester on Jewry Street. Winchester stories and imagery are stitched using innovative machine embroidery to create texture, tricks of scale and incredible colour.

The Southampton *Battle of Britain Lace* commemorates the Battle of Britain, Spitfires and Southampton's part in it and is on display at the Solent Sky Museum. It is over 3m high and was made by the lacemakers of Nottingham.

In the 1930s, Louisa Pesel, an international expert in design and stitch, and her artist friend, Sybil Blunt, were asked to create cushions and kneelers for the cathedral quire, altogether a huge project and the first of its kind. The Friends of Winchester Cathedral raised funds and over 200 volunteers were recruited and trained, becoming the Broderers of Winchester Cathedral. More than 600 items were produced all depicting elements of local history inspired by books in the Cathedral Library, the twelfth-century Winchester Bible and the Winchester School of Illumination. See them in the Winchester Cathedral quire today along with ancient and modern stitched altar frontals.

HAMPSHIRE'S WRITERS

Hampshire has been host and birthplace to some of literature's 'greats', some that were great in their time but have shrunk in stature, and some little-known but interesting writers.

Jane and Charlotte

Two women writing in the nineteenth century were entirely Hampshire women, living in the county nearly all their lives: Jane Austen and Charlotte Yonge. One you may have heard of, the other was equally if not more famous in her time.

Both were born in Hampshire to clergyman fathers: Jane in Steventon in 1775, Charlotte Mary Yonge in 1823 in Otterbourne. Charlotte had a stern and unconventional education provided by her father but she was also influenced by John Keble, leading light of the Oxford Movement, and rector in the neighbouring parish, Hursley. Jane was part of a large family, she attended schools in Southampton, Oxford and Reading but must have been influenced by her father too, who took in male school pupils to supplement his living.

Both began writing in their teens. For Jane, publishing her works was a struggle. Jane Austen scholar Claire Tomalin suggests that from the sales of all of her six novels, Jane would have received between £600 and £700 before her death, with perhaps an average of £40 a year. This never lifted her above the poverty line, which was set then at £55. In 2013, however, it was reported that *Pride and Prejudice* had sold 200 million copies in 200 years.

Charlotte's sales trajectory was the opposite, however. She wrote over 160 books, mainly novels. Her first success, *The Heir of Redclyffe* (1853), brought her fame and a large readership of people from all areas of society, including women and army officers. Even artists William Morris and Edward Burne-Jones read *The Heir of Redclyffe* aloud to each other while undergraduates at Oxford University and the hero Guy Morville's chivalric ideals inspired the Pre-raphaelite Brotherhood. At the time, Charlotte outsold Dickens and Thackeray. However, her books are out of print today, perhaps a little too moralistic for today's readership and unlikely to attract a TV adaptation.

Charlotte's profits were always ploughed back into church and charity causes (including a missionary ship), something her grandmother insisted on and was probably echoed by Yonge's own religious feelings.

Jane was very sociable and often stayed at friends' houses. In contrast, Charlotte was painfully shy and rarely ventured

Illustration from The Daisy Chain *by Charlotte Yonge. 'In a sort of impulse to do something for him, she took his hat from his hand.'*

far from her home, first Otterbourne House, then Elderfield, in Otterbourne.

Charlotte's novels were read and loved by many soldiers. *The Heir of Redclyffe* was particularly popular among officers serving in the Crimea in 1853. Jane's novels feature lots of soldiers, many of them cads and bad sorts. However, in a short story by Rudyard Kipling, 'The Janeites' (1926), it is First World War soldiers who are fans of Jane that form a Masonic Lodge, based on their shared love of her novels.

Neither woman married and both died in Hampshire.

Jane died in July 1817. In May 1817, Jane made her way to Hampshire's medical centre, Winchester, suffering with illness. She rented accommodation in College Street, No. 8, with her sister and was under the attention of Dr Giles Lyford (you can see his memorial in St Lawrence's Church, The Square, Winchester). However, unable to save her, she died in the house and six days later, on 24 July 1817, was buried in the cathedral.

Charlotte died in 1901. She is buried in Otterbourne Church, with a memorial also in the virginal enclave of the Lady Chapel, Winchester Cathedral. Jane lies in the North Aisle of the same cathedral surrounded by Rifle Brigade and other military memorials and perhaps, being by far the more sociable, is happy there. Jane wrote most of her books in Chawton, near Alton, and the house is now a museum.

During her lifetime, Charlotte Yonge had been asked to choose a name for a new parish to the south of Otterbourne, as a notable local resident and a donor of £500 to the church. It incorporated the villages of Eastley and Barton and she chose Eastley, but specified that it should be spelt Eastleigh as it was more modern. This is how the town spells its name today. Another legacy of Charlotte's is St Swithun's school in Winchester, the first girls' high school in the city. It was set up by two of her acolytes and hosts a scholarship in her name. The uniform features a daisy, in reference to Charlotte's novel *The Daisy Chain*.

There is a statue of Charlotte in Eastleigh railway station by Vivian Mallock and a statue of Jane in Basingstoke by Adam Roud.

POETS AND THEIR HAMPSHIRE INSPIRATIONS

Edward Thomas was inspired by the White Horse pub near Steep. The isolated pub, with its missing sign, inspired his first poem, 'Up in the Wind' (1914). From 1906 to his death in France in 1917, the celebrated poet lived, worked and was inspired by the village of Steep near Petersfield (and in fact much of Hampshire that he could walk and cycle through). He has a memorial stone on Shoulder of Mutton Hill and a memorial window in All Saints Church.

Alfred Tennyson was inspired by Wagonners Wells, a series of ponds in East Hampshire. 'Flower in the Crannied Wall' was composed by Tennyson in 1863 beside the wishing well there. The poem's underlying theme is the relationship between God, nature, and human life – all from a tiny flower growing at Waggoners Wells!

Robert Southey, a Romantic poet, was inspired by a Hampshire river and wrote 'For the Banks of the Hampshire Avon', beginning, 'A little while, O traveller! linger here, And let thy leisure eye behold and feel, The beauties of the place.'

John Keats, the Romantic poet, stayed in Winchester for only a short time in 1819, when he was beginning to suffer from 'consumption'. He said the air was worth 'sixpence a pint' and he liked the city, from which he took a walk most evenings across the water meadows to St Cross almshouses. It inspired one of the most famous and well-loved poems in the English language, 'Ode to Autumn', which begins with the famous line, 'season of mists and mellow fruitfulness …' You can take the same walk yourself in autumn and see what he meant.

Wulfstan was a Saxon monk at Winchester's Priory of St Swithun and produced, among other musical and literary works, a 3,400-line poem on the miracles of St Swithun, making him the first Winchester poet whose work we can read.

BRIEF SOJOURNS AND TENUOUS LINKS

Edmund Spenser, author of *The Faerie Queene*, lived at No. 1 Amery Street in Alton in 1590, when the first part of his epic was published. He returned to Ireland in 1591.

Alexander Pope (1688–1744), the poet and satirist, attended but was expelled from Twyford School. Another later-to-be-literary pupil at Twyford was Thomas Hughes, author of *Tom Brown's Schooldays*.

Charles Dickens was born in Portsmouth on 7 February 1812, his mother rushing in labour from an Old Beneficial Society Ball in Portsea to her home in Landport. The home, his birthplace, is now a museum. It might be a stretch to say Portsmouth influenced this best-selling of authors as he left eighteen months later and only returned once later in life. However, the infamous Andover workhouse perhaps inspired his depiction of these Victorian institutions and in his third novel his hero Nicholas Nickleby travels to Portsmouth to find work, where he is taken on as a playwright by Vincent Crummles. Also in this novel, Nicholas and Smike turn off the London to Portsmouth road, 12 miles short of Portsmouth, to a roadside inn. This is supposed to be Bottom Inn, now Bottom Cottage near Buriton.

Hampshire claims its own connection with Shakespeare through Titchfield Abbey. He is known to have stayed there with his patron, the third Earl of Southampton. It is suggested by some that *Romeo and Juliet* was even conceived there.

The faded name, Madame Doubtfire, above a long-gone rag and bone shop in Stockbridge, was the inspiration for *Madame Doubtfire* by novelist Anne Fine (later a film, *Mrs Doubtfire*).

Edward Gibbon, author of *The Decline and Fall of the Roman Empire*, lived at the Manor House in Buriton, but did not write his famous book there.

Geoffrey Chaucer of *Canterbury Tales* fame is one of the earliest of named authors, writing in the 1300s. He owned a manor at Ramridge, near the Weyhill Fair.

Elizabeth Gaskell, the Victorian novelist, bought a house on London Road in Holybourne, near Alton, to give to her husband when he retired. She kept it a secret until then, unsure if she could persuade him to leave Manchester. However, before the gift could be given, Elizabeth collapsed and died there on a visit with her daughters in November 1865.

Alice Pleasance Liddell, the little girl who was the inspiration for *Alice in Wonderland*, later lived in Lyndhurst, in the New Forest, under her married name Alice Hargreaves and became a society hostess. Her ashes were buried at St Michael and All Angels, Lyndhurst.

FICTIONALISED HAMPSHIRE

Thomas Hardy, Victorian novelist and poet, created a fictitious Wessex in his novels, centred on Dorset rather than Hampshire, but he thought of Hampshire as his 'Upper Wessex'. Winchester becomes Wintoncester in *Tess of the d'Urbevilles* and is where Tess is tried and eventually (spoiler alert) killed, with an accurate description of Romsey Road and the prison. He also stayed in the George Hotel, Winchester, in 1893 (where Barclays Bank now stands) with one of his female friends, Florence Henniker, and his poem 'At an Inn' describes that experience.

The fair at Weyhill appears in *The Mayor of Casterbridge* by Thomas Hardy as Weydon Priors fair. The novel's action opens with Henchard selling his wife at the fair. One may think that this never happened, but perhaps Hardy had heard of an incident that happened in 1832 when the annual register of the Weyhill fair records Joseph Thomson offering his wife for sale for 50 shillings. He didn't quite make that but accepted 20 shillings and a dog for her! Apparently all parties were content with the arrangement.

Portsmouth of the 1830s and '40s is depicted in *By Celia's Arbour* (1878) by Walter Besant, with some wonderful descriptions of the sea city and its old harbourside milieu.

Hyde's Drapery Emporium, Southsea, is in *Kipps* (1905) by H.G. Wells. The novel, although set in Folkestone, features a draper's assistant receiving an inheritance and must surely have been based on his experience as a draper's assistant in Southsea, which he described as 'indescribably tedious'.

King's Deverill, a fictional Hampshire village, is in *The Mating Season* (1949) by P.G. Wodehouse, a Jeeves and Wooster comedy, where Wooster is inveigled into performing in the village concert. Wodehouse, considered one of our best comedy writers, lived in Emsworth, at a house called Threepwood, between 1904 and 1913 and helped the boys at Emsworth House, a private school, with sports and swimming. He employed a housekeeper, Lilian

Hill, who he later described as the best friend he ever had and sent his regular column for a London newspaper by train every afternoon. Although called Belphur in the book, Emsworth features in *Damsel in Distress* during the time of the Great Oyster scare of 1902–06.

Exbury House, or HMS *Mastodon* as it was known in the Second World War, is in *Requiem for a Wren* by Nevil Shute, where he was stationed.

Grayshott is in *Heatherley* by Flora Thompson. This semi-autobiographical novel is the sequel to the more famous *Lark Rise to Candleford* trilogy. Thompson lived in Grayshott from 1898 to 1901. She worked as the telegraph operator in Grayshott post office, from where many writers who lived in the area would send telegrams. In 1916 she moved back to the Liphook area with her husband, staying until 1928. Liphook Library has a bust of her.

The Children of the New Forest (1847) by Captain Marryat was inspired by visits to his brother's stately home at Chewton Glen in the New Forest, and follows four orphan children during the Civil War who are helped by a verderer to escape Parliamentary forces and live in the forest. Marryat also describes the sinking of the *Royal George* at dock in Portsmouth (see Chapter 5, Disasters) in his story *Poor Jack*.

The Hampshire Downs are in *Watership Down* (1972) by Richard Adams. It follows a group of rabbits on their dangerous search for a new warren. You can find the real hill near Ecchinswell and other places that feature in the novel, such as Nuthanger Farm, Newtown Common and the River Test, are all real places nearby.

The River Itchen features in *The Water Babies* (1863) by Rev. Charles Kingsley, who was rector of Eversley and a frequent visitor to the Itchen at Itchen Abbas.

"Oh, you beautiful creature!"

Illustration from The Water Babies *by Charles Kingsley. By Alice B. Woodward.*

Winchester and Hampshire are the cathedral city of Barchester and county of Barsetshire in the novels by Anthony Trollope. Trollope attended Winchester College between 1827 and 1830. *The Warden* features an almshouse whose warden is receiving a larger income than he should and mirrored the real-life case of St Cross almshouses and its master, Francis North. The tiny church St Swithun-upon-Kingsgate in Winchester appears as St Cuthberts in the novel, too. Another book, *Ralph the Heir*, is set in north Hampshire, where Trollope's grandfather was vicar.

Winchester of the 1930s appears in *A Single Thread* (2019) by Tracy Chevalier. The novel features the Broderers of Winchester Cathedral.

Winchester College features in *Friendly Fire*, a strongly autobiographical novel by Patrick Gale, a Wykehamist (as former pupils of the college are known).

MORE HAMPSHIRE WRITERS

William Cobbett, writer of *Rural Rides* in the early 1820s, as well as numerous other works of journalism and political writings, lived in Botley from 1805. He gives us a wonderful insight into this county in the early nineteenth century through his travel writing.

The novelist Mary Russell Mitford was born in Alresford at 27 Broad Street, in 1787. She is best known for *Our Village*, a book of sketches of village life and characters.

The novelist Raymond Hitchcock lived in a converted mill in Abbots Worthy. His most successful novel was *Percy,* a rather risqué title about a penis transplant. Other books followed in the 1980s, including one set in Hampshire about the murder of King William Rufus in the New Forest in 1100. He was also an artist.

John Harmar was a very accomplished scholar and linguist and Warden of Winchester College. He played a major role in the translation and editing of the King James Bible, a huge influence on the English language.

Standing in front of the entrance to Winchester College and looking to the left, it is possible to see the windows of Harmar's study in which he worked on the Bible as one of the Oxford Company of translators. Lancelot Andrewes was Bishop of Winchester in 1618–26. Before he was bishop he was also involved in the translation. He was in the company of translators responsible for the first twelve books of the Old Testament and in effect the editorial director of the whole project. He was noted for his wise and powerful sermons and essays, and it was said by T.S. Eliot that he could 'take a word ... and derive ... the world from it'.

Lachlan MacKinnon, poet and writer, and his wife, another well-loved poet, Wendy Cope, lived at Winchester College while he was an English teacher there. He contributed to *Sixty-Six Books*, a set of plays at the Bush Theatre commemorating the 400th anniversary of the King James Bible (which, of course, was partly translated in Winchester College).

The Little White Horse by Elizabeth Goudge won the Carnegie medal for the best children's book of 1946. J.K. Rowling cites it as an influence on her Harry Potter series. Goudge partly lived in Barton-on-Sea and is buried there.

UNHAPPY LITERARY CHILDHOODS IN HAMPSHIRE

Rudyard Kipling, writer of *The Jungle Book*, the *Just So Stories* and the poem 'If', which was voted the nation's favourite in 2005 and 2009, spent an unhappy childhood in Portsmouth. Sent home from India by his parents, he lodged in Lorne Lodge, Campbell Road, Southsea with a very strict, not to say abusive, Mrs Holloway, who beat him regularly. Mr Holloway was a sea captain and had a scar, which was fascinating to Kipling and which he said had been gained when a whaling cable had pulled him under the waves and nearly taken his life.

Another one of the great Victorian novelists was William Makepeace Thackeray. Like Kipling later in the century, in 1817 he was sent back to England from India by his recently widowed mother to be educated. He attended the Southampton boarding school run by Alfred Arthur and his wife Rebecca from their house in the Polygon. Just like Kipling, it was not a happy time and involved beatings and abuse. However, trips to the Theatre Royal on French Street may have fired a love of the theatre.

In 1956, nearly 140 years after Jane Austen died there, another poet, playwright and novelist, Julia Darling, was born at No. 8 College Street in Winchester. One might not go so far to say she was unhappy but, finding the city stifling, she left in 1981 for the North-East. However, Winchester and her upbringing must have influenced her writing: her first novel, *Crocodile Soup* (1998), is partly set in the city and the main character lives in a house in which a Victorian poet, Harriet Smiles, had lived and died.

MODERN HAMPSHIRE NOVELISTS

Neil Gaiman, born in Portchester, is an award-winning author. His work includes *The Sandman* series of graphic novels, *Coraline* (2002), *The Graveyard Book* (2008) (heavily influenced by Rudyard Kipling's *The Jungle Book*), *American Gods* (2001) and *The Ocean at the End of the Lane* (2013), which was voted Book of the Year in the British National Book Awards.

Ian McEwan, born in Aldershot, is one of Hampshire's best-known novelists. His novels include *Atonement*, which was made into an Oscar-winning film. He has won many literary prizes and *The Times* named him one of fifty greatest British writers since 1945.

Claire Fuller lives, writes and teaches in Winchester and is a critically acclaimed novelist who won the prestigious Costa Novel Award 2021 for her novel *Unsettled Ground*. The judges described it as 'a beautiful and nuanced observation of the richness and pain of marginalised life'. It is set in the North Wessex Downs, in a fictional Hampshire village called Inkbourne. An earlier novel, *Bitter Orange*, was inspired by The Grange, near Alresford.

ACTORS AND FILMSTARS

Hampshire Hogs to Hollywood Hams

Kathleen Lockhart was born in 1894 at Southsea and emigrated to America in 1924 to appear in over thirty early films. Some of her film credits include *Brides are Like That* (1936), *The Devil is a Sissy* (1936), *Mother Wore Tights* (1947) and *Confidentially Connie* (1953).

Harry Stubbs was born in 1874 in Southampton but emigrated to America aged 16. He had a career on Broadway but moved to Hollywood in 1929 and took the lead in several films of the early 'sound' era: *The Invisible Man* (1933), *The Locked Door* (1929) and *Alibi* (1929).

Portsmouth-born H. Montagu Love was also winning roles in Hollywood films. He played opposite Rudolph Valentino, Errol Flynn and Lilian Gish, often as the heartless villain, a character for which he became known. In 1939's *Gunga Din*, Montagu Love reads the final stanza of Rudyard Kipling's original poem over the body of the slain Din.

Belita, born in Nether Wallop in 1923, was an Olympic figure skater and actress. She was born Maria Belita Jepson-Turner and competed in the 1936 Winter Olympics. She went on to Hollywood, where she skated and acted in films such as *Silver Skates* (1943) and *Lady Let's Dance* (1944). She could also ballet dance and perform underwater ballet.

Belita around 1948.

Bob Anderson was an Olympic fencer (representing Great Britain in Helsinki at the 1952 Olympics) born in Gosport in 1922 and also the best fight choreographer in Hollywood. He worked with actors such as Errol Flynn, Viggo Mortenson, Johnny Depp and Sean Connery on their sword-fighting scenes. During rehearsals with Errol Flynn for *The Master of Ballantrae*, he accidentally slashed Flynn's thigh. He worked on sword fights in *From Russia with Love*, the *Lord of the Rings* trilogy, *Pirates of the Caribbean: Curse of the Black Pearl*, *Highlander* and *The Princess Bride*. He also appeared as the stunt double for Darth Vader's fight scenes in the Star Wars films *The Empire Strikes Back* and *The Return of the Jedi*.

Frances Fisher was born in Milford-on-Sea and now works and lives in America. She has enjoyed a long theatre, TV and film career, including acting in *Unforgiven* with her then partner Clint Eastwood, and perhaps her most famous role as Rose's mother in *Titanic* (1999).

Boris Karloff created and played the definitive Hollywood *Frankenstein* (1931), but he also enjoyed cricket, gardening and lived in Bramshott between 1966 and 1969, at a house called Roundabout.

Variety, Farce and Comedy

Mark Melford was born George Smith in Portsmouth in 1850. He was a comic actor, playwright and variety artiste, working in Portsmouth in the late 1800s. He was often known by the soubriquet Rhymeo. He wrote drama, melodramas, comic sketches (including one called *A Hampshire Hog*, 1899), a musical drama and even a comic opera. From 1912 onwards he wrote and starred in silent films. He was a humanist, supporter of women's suffrage and actively opposed to cruelty towards performing animals. Indeed, he brought at least one case of cruelty to court, concerning performing elephants. He had a fondness for birds, especially jackdaws, jays and magpies. At his house, the Jackdaw's Nest on the outskirts of Southampton, a whole room was left just for his birds. *Non-suited* was his most popular comic sketch, in which he usually took the role of the barrister in a plot that involved a breach of promise suit. The provincial rights for the sketch were purchased for a then record price of £500 (perhaps £45,000 today). His daughter, Jackeydawra, was one of the first female filmmakers and a suffragette.

Alfred Hawthorne Hill was born in Southampton in 1924. He changed his name to Benny Hill and became a popular comedian, best known for *The Benny Hill Show*. It was exported to half the countries around the world and some surprising people were fans of his slapstick: in a June 2011 interview the American rapper Snoop Dogg said he was a fan. In 2006, Hill was voted seventeenth in ITV's poll of TV's fifty greatest stars by the British public. He was buried at Hollybrook Cemetery, Southampton in 1992. One might have thought grave robbing a thing of the past but during the night of 4 October 1992, following speculation in the media that Hill had been buried with a large amount of gold and jewellery, thieves excavated the grave and broke open the coffin. It is not known if anything was taken but the body was untouched. On discovery of the crime the grave was filled back in and as a security measure, a foot-thick concrete slab was placed over it.

Arthur English was born in Aldershot in 1919 and was a stage and TV actor and comedian, in the music hall tradition. His early-career comedy character was a 'spiv', where he would tell a long rambling story at a faster and faster pace until, at top speed, he ended with the catchphrase: 'Play the music! Open the cage!' He also appeared in sitcoms *Are you Being Served?* and *In Sickness and in Health*.

Comedian and actress Miranda Hart grew up in Petersfield. She is best known for her self-written sitcom *Miranda* and her role as Camilla Fortescue-Cholmondley-Brown, or Chummy, in *Call the Midwife*.

Peter Sellers was born in Castle Road, Southsea, and made his stage debut, aged two weeks, at the town's Kings Theatre with his parents. The family went on to tour provincial theatres with their variety act. He is best known for his work in *The Goon Show* with Harry Secombe, Spike Milligan and Michael Bentine in the 1950s and for his hilarious depiction of Inspector Clouseau in three *Pink Panther* films. He was recognised as a comic genius and a consummate lead actor and won the Bafta award for best actor in a lead role twice.

Nicholas Lyndhurst was not born in Lyndhurst, but instead in Emsworth. He is most well-known for his portrayal of Rodney, Del Boy's hapless brother in the sitcom *Only Fools and Horses*. He also starred in the time travel sitcom *Goodnight Sweetheart*.

Household Names from Hampshire
In the 1995 television adaptation of Jane Austen's *Pride and Prejudice*, Colin Firth plays Mr Darcy. He also played a Mr Darcy in *Bridget Jones's Diary,* a film with a plotline that has

a close resemblance to *Pride and Prejudice* but set in modern times. Firth grew up in Hampshire, at Grayshott, and went to school in Winchester, at the Montgomery of Alamein Secondary School (now Kings School).

Martin Freeman became a household name after his 'romantic hero' role of Tim in the hit sitcom *The Office*. He went on to play Dr Watson in BBC TV's *Sherlock* and subsequently the titular character in the film trilogy based on J.R.R. Tolkien's book, *The Hobbit*. He was born in Aldershot.

Tommy Jessop was the first actor with Down's syndrome to star in a prime time drama, *Line of Duty*. He toured theatres as the first professional actor with Down's to play Hamlet and the first to become a voting member of Bafta. Jessop started at the Blue Apple Theatre group in Winchester, which his parents set up for young people with learning difficulties.

A perhaps less recognised actor is Nicholas Briggs, who was born in Lyndhurst in 1961, but you might recognise his voice. He has provided voices for the long-running BBC TV programme *Doctor Who,* most famously the Daleks and the Cybermen.

THE MUSIC OF HAMPSHIRE

Seven Hampshire Hymn Writers
Isaac Watts, one of our finest hymn writers, lived in Southampton and the Civic Centre clock there still chimes the first notes of his most famous hymn, 'O God, Our Help in Ages Past', every four hours. The view from Eling churchyard across the Test apparently inspired the hymn 'There is a Land of Pure Delight'.

Anne Steele was born in Broughton in 1717 and lost her fiancé when he drowned on the day of her wedding. Her output perhaps reflects her tragedy. She wrote 144 hymns.

Thomas Ken was a cleric who attended Winchester College and was a canon at Winchester Cathedral, where he famously refused to put up King Charles II's mistress Nell Gwynne when the royal court visited. As a hymn writer he has had few equals in England and he wrote 'Praise God From Whom All Blessings Flow', 'Awake, My Soul, and With the Sun' and 'Glory to Thee, My God, this Night', which are still well known.

John Keble, leader of the high-church Oxford Movement, vicar of Hursley and friend to novelist Charlotte Yonge, also wrote hymns and many appeared in his book *The Christian Year.* They are still sung today, such as 'New Every Morning'.

Thomas Weelkes was an English madrigal composer in the late 1500s, well known for his church compositions. He was likely born at Elsted, near Petersfield, and was organist at Winchester Cathedral from 1598.

Samuel Sebastian Wesley was a composer and organist at Winchester Cathedral and Winchester College (from 1849). Of his hymn tunes the best known are 'Aurelia' and 'Hereford'. He has a memorial tablet in Winchester Cathedral and his house can be seen on Kingsgate Street.

Organ music has a very long history in Winchester. This is what Wulfstan says about the organ in New Minster in the 990s:

> Twice six bellows above are ranged in a row, and fourteen lie below. These, by alternate blasts, supply an immense quantity of wind, and are worked by seventy strong men, labouring with their arms, covered with perspiration, ... Like thunder the iron tones batter the ear, so that it may receive no sound but that alone. To such an amount does it reverberate, echoing in every direction, that everyone stops with his hands to his gaping ears, being in no wise able to draw near and bear the sound, which so many combinations produce. The music is heard throughout the town.

Wulfstan himself, as well as being a poet and writer, was a musician and held the position of precentor, effectively leader of musical worship at the Old Minster, Winchester, in the 900s. He was one of the earliest writers of church music, including hymns, Mass settings and chants, and he wrote many of these down in one of the earliest and largest collections of church music, *The Winchester Troper*. This manuscript of 160 chants dates from around 1000 CE and uses both notation and two-part musical settings (ornamental harmonies to Gregorian plainchant).

Rock, Punk, Folk

Robyn Hitchcock is a singer-songwriter, son of Raymond Hitchcock and friend of Julia Darling (see More Hampshire Writers for both), for whom he wrote 'Underground Sun'. Another song is called 'Winchester'. Hitchcock wrote the song 'Sunday Never Comes' for the 2018 film *Juliet, Naked*, which was sung in the movie by Ethan Hawke's character, an aging, reclusive musician. Hitchcock lived in Abbots Worthy and attended Winchester College.

Carl Barat, the co-frontman and co-founder (with Pete Doherty) of the band The Libertines and guitarist and frontman of Dirty Pretty Things, was born in Basingstoke in 1978 and grew up in Whitchurch. The Libertines regularly hit the headlines, often due to Doherty's drug addictions. Barat continues to make music as a solo artist and with various bands including the supergroup The Bottletop Band and The Jackals. He was awarded an honorary degree from the University of Winchester in 2012 for his contribution to the arts.

Frank Turner is a singer-songwriter playing acoustic punk/folk music who has released eight solo albums and enjoyed worldwide success. He began life though in Winchester and Meonstoke where he grew up. His song 'Wessex Boy' is about coming home to Winchester. The lyrics mention Jewry Street, the Railway Inn music venue and the Cathedral Close, and the video features many Winchester landmarks including the Buttercross, Cathedral Close, the King Alfred statue and High Street (it also, incidentally, prominently shows a band member reading *Folklore of Hampshire,* another The History Press publication). In 2014, Turner appeared on the BBC's *Celebrity Mastermind* with specialist subject Iron Maiden and won with twenty points.

Andy Burrows, born in Winchester, gained fame as the drummer in the band Razorlight in the noughties. Burrows co-wrote the hits 'America' and 'Before I Fall to Pieces', and has released solo albums including *The Colour of My Dreams* (2008) for Naomi House, a hospice for children in Winchester. He also plays and writes with We Are Scientists, Smith & Burrows (with Editors' frontman Tom Smith) and Tom Odell.

Jon Boden is a fiddle player and is best known for being lead composer and performer in folk band Bellowhead. He is also one half of Spiers and Boden and has received eleven BBC2 Radio Folk Awards. He grew up in Winchester and has noted his formative experiences as including: Winchester during the time of the Twyford Down protesters trying to prevent the M3 coming through with folk players busking in the High Street; seeing the Levellers play at Winchester's Hat Fair; Irish piper Liam O'Flynn at the Tower Arts Centre; and playing at the Southampton folk sessions.

Laura Marling was born in Eversley in north Hampshire, and is a critically acclaimed folk singer-songwriter, producing 'nu-folk' music. Several of her albums have been nominated for the Mercury Prize.

7

HAMPSHIRE PEOPLE

HAMPSHIRE SAINTS AND THEIR QUIRKY MIRACLES

The most well-known saint of Hampshire and its patron saint is St Swithun (died around 863 CE). In life he was Bishop of Winchester and perhaps tutor to King Alfred. In death he was an incredibly popular medieval saint for pilgrimages. His remains were held in a rich shrine in, first, Old Minster, then the Norman Winchester Cathedral. Today you can see a memorial in the East End of the cathedral where his shrine used to be before Henry VIII's men came to destroy it in 1539. The memorial incorporates a set of broken eggs and some apple trees, and these refer to miracles of his. One such miracle was the mending of broken eggs when a lady dropped them on the City Bridge on the way to market. He also had the bridge built and so he is often portrayed holding a bridge (as in Winchester Cathedral's Great Screen). It is said that if 15 July (St Swithun's Day) is fair then the weather will be fair for forty days and forty nights; if foul, then it will be foul for forty days and nights. His weather-predicting powers come from his feast day in 974 CE when he was removed from his resting place outside Old Minster to be processed round the city and repositioned in a rich shrine inside the church. It is said the forty-day storm that ensued was Swithun's displeasure.

*The apple harvest is good if the weather is wet
at the end of the summer.*

Apparently the apple harvest
is particularly good when the
late summer weather includes
lots of rain – hence the apples on
his memorial.

St Ethelflaeda was a nun of noble birth
at Romsey Abbey in the 900s. She is said to have
read the lesson at matins by having her finger glow
like a light, when her candle blew out. She also had a penchant
for sneaking out at night and standing in a stream (perhaps the
Test) reading the psalms. All very pious. She died in 1016 but it
was said miracles happened at her tomb, so she was brought into
a shrine in the church. Her feast day is 23 October.

St Edburga was also an Anglo-Saxon noblewoman, daughter
of King Edward the Elder. She had been placed as a child in
Nunnaminster Abbey in Winchester after her holy ways had
been noticed. There she was said to clean the other nuns' shoes
anonymously at night. She died in 960 CE and became a very
popular saint with a big silver and gold shrine at Nunnaminster
and a feast day on 15 June.

St Birinus converted King Cynegils of Wessex to Christianity
in around 634 CE and started to build the first church at
Winchester, kick-starting Christianity in the kingdom and in
Hampshire. His remains were brought to Winchester Cathedral
and he retained a shrine there until Bishop Thomas Langton died
of plague in 1501 and Birinus was evicted to make way for his
chantry chapel. At the east end, however, you can see the Birinus
cross, which contains a piece of stone from his original shrine at
Dorchester-on-Thames in Oxfordshire.

St Aethelwold was chiefly important for the PR he did for
that other saint, Swithun. He was also Bishop of Winchester,

but 100 years later from 963 CE. He was the one who removed Swithun from his original resting place, risking his wrath through long thunderstorms. However, he also extended the Old Minster and built a magnificent shrine in which he placed the body and increased Swithun's popularity tenfold. On St Aethelwold's feast day prayers are said for 'rebuilder of the second minster, maker of the conduits, lover of music', as he built a stone conduit for the monastery to bring fresh water and flush away waste, called the Lockburn. He also introduced the rule of St Benedict to the monastery at the Minster and, for that reason, he is often portrayed with a book – the book of the Rule of St Benedict. His feast day is 1 August.

Hedda was Bishop of Winchester under King Ine of Wessex and was the first to move the cathedral church of the Diocese from Dorchester-on-Thames to Winchester. The soil around his grave was said to heal humans and animals when mixed with water and a large pit appeared near to his grave as a consequence.

St Waltheof's bones are not in Hampshire but he was killed here. He was a rebellious Anglo-Saxon nobleman under William the Conqueror. He was initially allowed to keep his lands after the Norman Conquest, but later rebelled – twice. This was not advisable. He was taken to the top of St Giles Hill in Winchester to be beheaded in the dead of night. He asked to say the Lord's prayer, but the axeman, getting impatient, chopped off his head before he could finish. As his head rolled down the hill to Bubb's Cross it was heard to be still reciting the prayer. His body was later recovered and went to Crowland Abbey in Lincolnshire, where he became a saint.

THE MEDICS

Alured Clarke founded the first County Hospital in 1736, later to become the Royal Hampshire County Hospital on Romsey Road in Winchester. A canon of Winchester Cathedral, he raised funds from the great and good of the county and opened the hospital on the corner of Colebrook Street, now a car park. He believed most illness resulted from un-Christian living and the painted words over the lintel of the entrance of that first hospital explain his viewpoint: 'Despise thou not the chastening of the Almighty'. Each patient was given books on religious instruction and 'laid under such restrictions, as may, by degrees, recover them out of that profligate State of Life'. The hospital treated those suffering from dropsy, rheumatism, paralysis and scorbutic cases, as well as the lame. From small beginnings it became a medical centre attracting excellent doctors.

Bald's Leechbook was an early Anglo-Saxon book of remedies, written around 900 in Winchester, probably at the cathedral scriptorium. It is the oldest-surviving medical book in any western European vernacular language. In addition to injuries and infections, some of its remedies address supernatural problems: one is against elves (*ælfcynne*), others for night goblin visitors (*nihtgehgan*) and devils (*deofol*). The manuscript takes its name from *læca*, the Old English word for physician. This word later became associated with the leeches that were used for bloodletting in pre-modern medicine. Mostly the treatments call for herbs but one requires a porpoise:

> In case a man be a lunatic; take skin of a mereswine or porpoise, work it into a whip, swinge the man therewith, soon he will be well. Amen. (III, xl)

But please don't try this at home!

Florence Nightingale is associated with the county because her family's country seat was at Embley Park and she is buried at West Wellow Church. She famously revolutionised and professionalised nursing, but her real skill was in management and organisation. She was the go-to advisor and turned her – usually critical – eye on many hospitals upon her return from the Crimean War, even though she was debilitated by an illness she had contracted in the Crimea. These projects included the rebuilding of Winchester's Royal Hampshire County Hospital on Romsey Road and Netley Military Hospital. She was ruthless, yet charming when she needed to be, when persuading those in power of what needed to change. She was also brilliant at maths and statistics, compiling visual reports in an innovative way to effect change in nursing and hospitals. She loved cats and was said to have owned over sixty in her ninety-year life, which she named after prominent men such as Disraeli, Gladstone and Bismarck and fed from china plates.

POLITICIANS

Winchester College, one of the foremost public schools in the country, has produced six Chancellors of the Exchequer: Henry Addington (1801–10), Robert Lowe, Viscount Sherbrooke (1868–73), Stafford Cripps (1947–50), Hugh Gaitskill (1950–51), Geoffrey Howe (1979–83) and Rishi Sunak (2020–22) but only one Prime Minister: Henry Addington again (1801–04). He was appointed Prime Minister and Chancellor of the Exchequer at the same time. He was described as having 'the indefinable air of a village apothecary inspecting the tongue of the State' by Rosebery and was not a very popular or colourful PM.

James Callaghan, Labour Prime Minister in 1976–79, is a Hampshire Hog, being born and brought up in Portsmouth, with a naval family background.

Another Wykehamist who achieved a certain success in his career at court was Thomas Coryat, who became court jester to King James I.

SPIES

Commander Lionel 'Buster' Crabb was known as one of the best Navy divers in the 1940s and '50s. He undertook several top secret and dangerous diving missions to gain intelligence for Britain. He was also a hard drinker with reckless regard for his life – probably what was needed for a diving spy in those days. There was one mission from which he never returned, however. The Navy denied he was on official business, but he was seen diving around the Russian ship *Ordzhonikidze*, which was in Portsmouth delivering Russian leaders for goodwill talks in 1956. It was a fragile time in relations and spying on the revolutionary design of the cruiser could have ruined the talks. The Navy gave out the news that he had drowned at Portsmouth while testing 'certain underwater apparatus', but his death remained a mystery for many years. Had Crabb's fitness failed him after years of heavy drinking? Did the Russians discover him? Did something go wrong with the dive? Did he defect to the Soviets? His body was apparently found months later in Chichester Harbour, although it was only his personal diving suit that was identifiable. An ex-Soviet agent claimed in the 1990s that Crabb was seen and shot while surfacing from his underwater mission.

Peter Mews was Bishop of Winchester in 1684–1706, but this churchman had another life as a secret agent and a master of disguise. He began his career as a soldier and an army chaplain, and he spied initially for the Royalists during the Civil War, using the code name 757. He worked secretly to bring about the restoration of King Charles II and was rewarded with first the Bishopric of Bath and Wells, and then Winchester. He was still fighting battles when nearing 70, when he took an active part in the Battle of Sedgemoor in 1685. He wore a large black patch on his left cheek as a result of a facial injury on the battlefield. His memorial is in the Guardian Angels Chapel in Winchester Cathedral.

Another intelligence officer called Peter, who lived close by, near Winchester Cathedral Close, three centuries later, was Peter Smithers. He worked for naval intelligence in America, France and Mexico during the Second World War. He later became a respected botanist and landscape gardener as well as a politician and MP for Winchester. He was friends with Ian Fleming, writer of the James Bond novels. Indeed Smithers's wife, an American heiress, owned a gold typewriter, which has led to him being suspected as an inspiration for James Bond himself.

A HISTORY OF HAMPSHIRE THROUGH WILLIAMS

You could tell almost all the history of Hampshire with the various Williams that have lived here. Bishops, kings, writers and eccentrics – some have changed the course of Hampshire history, some have just added a bit of colour to the story.

William is a French name and the first came here from Normandy when he invaded. **William the Conqueror** built a huge castle at Winchester, as well as a new cathedral and new abbey buildings. He commissioned an inventory (Domesday Book) and a history of his invasion by the victorious side (Bayeaux Tapestry), both of which may have been compiled and made in Winchester. He came to Winchester to 'wear his crown' every Easter in a ceremony in the Old Minster (his new cathedral was unfinished), a piece of Norman PR in the most Anglo-Saxon of cities.

William Walkelin was a Norman appointed by William the Conqueror as bishop to build his cathedral. He made the longest nave in the world at the time and sneakily relieved William the Conqueror of all the wood in his forest, Hampage Wood, to build it.

William II or Rufus also 'wore his crown' at Winchester and gave the right to hold the great Fair of St Giles to the Bishop of Winchester. He was killed in the New Forest (see Chapter 4, Journeys).

Bishop of Winchester **William Edington** steered Hampshire through the Black Death (although his suggestion of gathering in Winchester's Square to sing penitential psalms may have done more harm than good!). He began the remodelling of Winchester Cathedral, but it was cut short by that pandemic.

William of Wykeham was Bishop of Winchester in 1366–1404 and is a Hampshire son with an incredible rags-to-riches story. Born into a humble family in Wickham in 1324, he rose to become the most powerful man in the kingdom, bar perhaps the king: it was said by Froissart that 'everything was done by him and nothing was done without him'. He was talent-spotted and educated at the priory school in Winchester, then went on to catch the king's eye and was made Surveyor of the King's Work – effectively project manager and architect in one – working on Windsor Castle. At the age of 42 he was offered the Bishopric of Winchester and at the same time became the chief advisor to the king, the Chancellor. The Bishopric of Winchester was the richest in the land, with an income from a number of estates all over the south-east and south-west of the country. He spent that money doing up his multiple houses, including at Wolvesey and Bishop's Waltham, giving royal hospitality, including for King Henry IV's wedding, and founding New College, Oxford, and a school, Winchester College. He also completely remodelled Winchester Cathedral in the Perpendicular Gothic style with huge, magnificent new windows. His motto 'Manners Makyth Man', still the motto of Winchester College today, reminds us that it is not birth or rank that make a man but his manners, morals or talents.

William Wynford, master mason and ingenious architect. He worked on Wykeham's projects of Winchester College and Winchester Cathedral – replacing the three sets of Norman arches with two sets of Gothic ones all down the nave, without rebuilding it. Clever guy!

Master William, the king's painter, decorated the Guardian Angels Chapel and **William Lyngwode** carved the amazing quire stalls. The merchant with a falcon, acrobats, green men, townspeople and peering heads at the ends of the spandrels are perhaps all depictions of various and vivacious residents of Winchester in the 1300s.

William Walker saved the cathedral from falling down 500 years after Wykeham, between 1906 and 1911, by diving underneath the walls quite literally and helping lay proper foundations in the incredibly high water table that was threatening the walls. Hopefully he ensured it will stand for another 1,000 years. Incidentally, his assistant was another William, **William West**. After helping with the cathedral, West ran a fish shop in Winchester for a number of years.

William Soper was merchant, MP and first shipbuilder of Southampton. When the king, Henry V, decided to build ships at Southampton, Soper was the obvious choice, not least because he had capital of his own from his merchant activities. He built and adapted ships at Hamble, Bursledon and Southampton, including *Grace Dieu* in 1418, the largest ship of its day. He was appointed Keeper and Governor of the King's Ships in 1420. One could say the shipbuilding industry of Hampshire began with him.

William Paulet was the first Marquess of Winchester, created so by Queen Elizabeth I. He had previously served as the Surveyor of the King's Widows and Governor of Idiots! He sat in the courts that tried both Queen Anne Boleyn and Thomas More, during the time of accusations, intrigue and beheadings surrounding King Henry VIII's court. When asked how he survived these dangerous times he replied: 'I was born of the willow, not of the oak,' meaning he was flexible and ready to bend with the needs of the circumstance. Queen Elizabeth noted that she could easily have married him as she liked him so much, if he wasn't quite so old!

Hayling Island was only reachable by a ford before 1824, when a bridge was built. It was called the Wadeway or the

Horse Road to low water. The Hayling Island railway was opened in 1867, crossing to the island on a wooden bridge. The little tank engines that used to make the crossing were known as 'Hayling Billys'.

William Joliffe and **King William III** were at Petersfield. The former left money in his will in 1750 to make a statue of the latter. This was done and even gilded. It was moved from his home at Petersfield House in 1812, was bought by the council in 1911, restored and now resides in the centre of Petersfield today. King William III also gets the Roman treatment in his still-gilded and very bright statue at Portsmouth Historic Dockyard. This time given by Richard Norton, supporter of Cromwell.

William Gilpin was an influential artist of the late 1700s and Reverend of Boldre, in the New Forest, from 1777. He was creator of the 'picturesque' method of drawing, a set of rules for depicting nature, which became popular in the 1700s with young people touring Britain and the Continent. The 'rules' were sometimes satirised, even at the time. For example, Elizabeth Bennet, in Jane Austen's *Pride and Prejudice,* refuses to join Mr Darcy and the Bingley sisters at one point with the observation, 'You are charmingly group'd, and ... the picturesque would be spoilt by admitting a fourth.' He was an enlightened educationalist too and when headmaster at Cheam School he instituted a system of fines rather than corporal punishments and encouraged the pupils to keep gardens and shops! He is buried and has a monument in St John's Church, Boldre.

William Jacob and **William Johnson** first adorned the *Hampshire Chronicle* on 27 September 1813. The paper has been running since 1772 and is therefore one of the longest-running in the country. These brothers-in-law took it over after training on it as printing apprentices. They printed simultaneously from their two premises in Gosport (under the name Johnson and Jacob) and at 98 (now 57) High Street, Winchester (under the name Jacob and Johnson). It flourished under their leadership and they had a distribution as far as Fareham and Lymington. Two more generations of the families continued to take the paper from strength to strength until 1919. Their premises, where the printing press was located and where Jacob lived and raised his ten children, can still be seen today at the top of Winchester High Street, bearing their names above beautiful Georgian bow windows. The inside is now an Italian restaurant. The paper hasn't moved far, though; it currently resides on Upper Brook Street, just a few metres away.

A character of old Southsea in the 1800s was '**Billy the Clown**', a preacher on Southsea Common. His sad life story involved an early period working as a clown in Cook's Circus on the corner of Chandos and Buckingham Streets, but after a fire broke out and killed all the animals Billy became very depressed. He turned to drink and beating his wife. But his life was turned around by Rev. Rose of the King Street Chapel. Billy gave up the drink and devoted his life to preaching on Southsea Common.

William Cornwallis-West, owner of the Newlands estate at Milford and promoter of the village as a premier seaside resort, added the last two words to Milford-on-Sea's name in 1886. He planned a pier, railway station, public baths, health spa and golf course, but lack of funds, and indeed interest, led to its failure.

W.T. Stead (or William Thomas Stead) was a journalist and social reformer. Although born in Northumberland, he spent his last years in South Hayling (30 Selsmore Road) from 1895. He was hugely influential in the late 1800s and very energetic with a powerful personality. He developed 'government through journalism' and campaigned on issues such as child prostitution, slums, the Contagious Diseases Act, peace, and a 'High Court of Justice among the Nations'. He was nominated for the Nobel Peace Prize several times. He was a pioneer in investigative journalism and, in order to prove his revelations about child prostitution, he arranged to 'purchase' 13-year-old Eliza Armstrong from her father, a chimney sweep. His subsequent article in his paper *The Pall Mall Gazette* changed hands for twenty times their original value. A daring escapade, which helped expose the terrible exploitation, it nonetheless landed him in prison for three months for the purchase itself! He also pioneered the use of what we would call 'tabloid' journalism – he employed huge headlines (the first to use 24-point with the headline TOO LATE! on the front page when the Gordon Relief Expedition failed at Khartoum), and also broke up the text with diagrams, maps and sub-headings. He was a spiritualist, believing he could communicate with the dead, and spoke and wrote Esperanto. Stead died in the *Titanic* disaster in 1912, eerily having written an article several years before on the consequence of a ship sinking with not enough lifeboats for passengers.

W.H. Hudson was a naturalist and author, hailing originally from Argentina. He was a leading prose writer of his day and an influential early environmental campaigner. Amongst his works is *Hampshire Days* (1903), which describes his experiences in Hampshire, including the New Forest and Itchen and Test valleys. The Hampshire village of Martin was his Winterbourne Bishop in *A Shepherd's Life*. One can find the grave of William Lawes (died 1886) in the graveyard of Martin Church, the inspiration for the character Isaac Bawcombe in the book.

OUTSTANDING ARTHURS

Arthur Wellesley, Duke of Wellington, hero of Waterloo in 1815, was rewarded with a house and estate in Hampshire at Stratfield Saye after the battle. He was also Lord Lieutenant of Hampshire (1820–52). Perhaps the best way to understand what Wellington did at Waterloo is to visit the Rifles Museum in Peninsula Barracks, Winchester, where there is an incredibly detailed and dramatic diorama of the Battle of Waterloo with a sound and light display.

Prince Arthur, son of King Henry VII and Elizabeth of York, was born at the Priory of St Swithun in Winchester, in 1486 – deliberately. His father wished him to be born in the city he believed was Camelot, legendary city of King Arthur. Note that the baby prince was named after the fabled king, too. Henry VII believed his family, the Tudors, were descended from King Arthur. The little prince had a lot to live up to! He was betrothed to a Spanish princess, Katharine of Aragon, at the age of 2.

Katharine was barely 16 when she endured thirty-three days of travel by sea and land in 1501 to meet her husband-to-be at Dogmersfield, near Fleet. After initial problems, when the Spanish party prevented the groom's party from meeting the princess, both Henry VII, her future father-in-law and Prince Arthur spent several days getting to know Katharine. The royal party left for London and the pair were married at St Paul's Cathedral on 14 November 1501.

Sadly, Arthur died soon after his marriage in 1502 and his brother Henry became king and married Katharine, Arthur's widow. King Henry VIII also believed in King Arthur and that his great round table adorned the wall of the Great Hall at Winchester Castle. At a grand feast to be held for the visiting King Charles V of Spain, he arranged for the table to be restored and painted with an image of King Arthur and the names of the twenty-four knights. After a few repaints it remains there today. However, we now know that the table dates back to around the 1280s, King Edward I's time. As another believer in King Arthur and Winchester as his Camelot, Edward had commissioned the table for an Arthurian tournament and feast.

A manuscript copy of Malory's *Le Morte d'Arthur*, written in 1469, was found after many centuries in Winchester College's archives. In 1934, the assistant headmaster Walter Oakeshott was looking for interesting book bindings when he discovered this manuscript in a safe. No one knows where it originally came from, but it had been sitting there unknown in the very city thought to be Camelot. It is the only known manuscript form of the stories of King Arthur from soon after Malory's death.

Arthur Conan Doyle, best known for his Sherlock Holmes stories and novel *The Lost World*, began his working life as a doctor in Portsmouth, at Elm Grove, Southsea, where he created Sherlock Holmes and wrote *A Study in Scarlet* and *The Sign of Four*. He was also the first goalkeeper of the team that was a forerunner of Portsmouth Football Club. By the time he left the town in 1890 he was an acclaimed writer. He later bought a house, Bignell Wood, in Minstead, in the New Forest, which he and his wife used as a rural retreat, and he is buried in Minstead graveyard.

Conan Doyle lived near Hindhead at one time and was a regular in Flora Thompson's post office in Grayshott. She describes how 'scarcely a day passed without his bursting like a breeze into the post office, almost filling it with his fine presence and the deep tones of his jovial voice. As he went through the village he had a kindly greeting for all, rich and poor, known and unknown alike. He was probably the most popular man in the neighbourhood.'

There are several mentions of Hampshire in Conan Doyle's stories. He used a Winchester hotel, The Black Swan, in his Holmes story *The Mystery of the Copper Beeches*. It is here that Holmes meets the protagonist Violet Hunter. The hotel was demolished in the 1930s but you can still see a figure of a black swan where it stood on the corner of Southgate Street and the High Street, Winchester. In *Silver Blaze*, Holmes and Watson head to Winchester racecourse, in reality located on Worthy Down, just outside Winchester, for the denouement where the missing racehorse is revealed. In *The Problem of Thor Bridge* (1927) a maid, Grace Dunbar, is held for murder in Winchester Gaol, where Holmes and Watson visit her. She has been working at an American financier's Hampshire estate, where the murder occurred. This estate is less easy to place and may be fictional.

The Black Swan Hotel in Winchester in the nineteenth century.
This hotel is where Violet Hunter meets Holmes and Watson in The
Mystery of the Copper Beeches. *(© 2021 Winchester City Council,*
provided by Hampshire Cultural Trust)

Lastly, in *A Study in Scarlet*, Dr Watson recounts his earlier life
before meeting Holmes and reveals he trained at Netley Hospital
as an Army surgeon.

Admiral Arthur Philip was the first Governor of New South
Wales, founder of Sydney and modern Australia. Australia
Day is celebrated on 26 January and this is the day Captain
Philip claimed Sydney Cove for Britain after his long voyage.
He had been selected as the leader of the First Fleet of eleven
ships to leave Portsmouth in 1787, full of convicts sentenced
to transportation. He set up a farming colony to truly settle
with British people the land that Captain Cook had discovered.
His naval career had prepared him well for the voyage and he
managed to accurately navigate 15,063 nautical miles with only
thirty-one deaths, an excellent outcome for the time. However,
it was the skills he learned while running a small farm on less

than premium soil at Lyndhurst in the New Forest that enabled him to create a successful settlement, growing their own food, raising animals, creating social and legal structures and a hope of freedom for the convicts. He was assisted by the very able Edward Dodd, his farm servant at Lyndhurst, who led on all agricultural matters.

Arthur Brandon was an eccentric activist who capitalised on the lifting of the government's ban on tobacco growing after 250 years, in 1910. He attempted to grow his own tobacco on a commercial scale at Church Crookham between 1911 and 1937, became the president of the British Tobacco Growers' Association and argued against government red tape. He experimented with thirty varieties of tobacco, settling on Samos and Blue Pryor. The process was labour intensive and involved hand weeding, topping the terminal buds, harvesting, wilting in the sun, curing with oak smoke over six weeks, striping, grading and bundling (rehandling), then drying, softening with steam and finally packing into barrels. Commercial tobacco growing didn't survive but it wasn't through want of promotion by Brandon, who became rather a press and radio star.

HENRYS OF HAMPSHIRE

Henrys are almost as prolific as Williams in Hampshire's history. Here are a few of them.

King Henry I got his crown by being single-minded in the face of crisis. When his brother, King William II, was killed in the New Forest by the glancing blow of an arrow, Henry did not stay to administer first aid, but rode full tilt to Winchester Castle to claim crown and treasury of the kingdom. He became king in 1100 and ruled until 1135, when he died, causing a succession crisis that led to another Henry coming to the fore ...

Henri de Blois had a big impact on the county through his position as Bishop of Winchester. He was grandson to William the Conqueror, nephew of Henry I, brother to King Stephen (male but not Henry I's rightful heir) and cousin to Empress Matilda (female, daughter of Henry I and the rightful heir). That put him right in the middle of the Civil War that ensued, the Anarchy of 1138 to 1153. In 1141, Henri organised an impressive ceremony in Winchester Cathedral to name Empress Matilda 'Lady of the English' (nearly Queen but not quite!) but he later withdrew his support. His double-crossing led to a huge siege called the Rout of Winchester and the burning of much of the city in August 1141. However, he was also responsible for building quite a lot, too: he founded the almshouses of St Cross, which was much needed after the war, Wolvesey Palace (the Bishop's Palace), Bishop's Waltham Palace and Merdon Castle, and he commissioned the Winchester Bible.

King Henry II was the first of the Plantagenet kings, son of Empress Matilda, and he came to Hampshire several times. First, during the Anarchy, in 1153 to draw up and sign the Treaty of Winchester with King Stephen, which ensured he inherited the crown of England after Stephen. It was sealed with a 'kiss of peace' in Winchester Cathedral. He came back when Stephen had died to claim his new throne, landing in the New Forest due to bad weather and receiving the homage of his nobles at Winchester Castle. It is said they 'trembled like reeds in the wind' to meet him.

Young Henry was the son of Henry II and was crowned at Winchester Cathedral in 1172 in an unusual coronation where he was not king at the end of it. The event was organised even before his father was dead in an effort to ensure the succession. However, it didn't work because, in the end, he died before his father, so he never did become King Henry III.

The real **King Henry III** was King John's son. He was born and christened in Winchester and his nickname was Henry of Winchester. He became king in 1216 when he was only 9 years old and his kingdom had been taken over by barons and the French Prince Louis. But luckily for him the Bishop of

Winchester, Peter des Roches, was on hand to help him through his duties. He had a long reign, until 1272, and spent a record eighteen royal Christmases at Winchester. He also liked to spend money – lots of it, which he often gained with loans from the Jewish community. He spent a record amount on Winchester Castle, repairing it to the tune of £10,000.

King Henry IV married his second wife, Joan of Navarre, in 1403 at Winchester Cathedral, with the wedding feast at the Bishop's Palace.

Henry V mustered a force of around 12,000 men at Portchester Castle before sailing for France and the Battle of Agincourt. He boarded his ship *Le Trinite* somewhere between Southampton and Portsmouth. Before his invasion, Henry had held diplomatic talks with the French ambassadors in July 1415 at the Bishop of Winchester's Palace (the bishop was also his uncle, Henry Beaufort). They were unable to reach a compromise, Beaufort being rather bullish about the English demands, and war continued.

Henry Beaufort was Bishop of Winchester (1404–47), Cardinal and Lord Chancellor to King Henry V. He was related to three royal Henrys: brother to King Henry IV, uncle to King Henry V and great-uncle to King Henry VI. He was extremely powerful, particularly under the boy King Henry VI's reign, when he took control of government and financed the state and its wars with high-interest loans. His tomb or chantry chapel is the richest one in Winchester Cathedral, but it also took the most damage from Parliamentarians in the 1640s as

King Henry VI, who married Margaret of Anjou at Titchfield Abbey.

he was a member of the royal family. He financed the Great Screen in Winchester Cathedral.

Margaret of Anjou sailed into Portchester on 9 April 1445 amid a terrific thunderstorm. Despite the storm, the villagers still strewed the streets with rushes and cheered loudly. Perhaps as a result of the storm, the princess became ill but she recovered in time to meet and marry her husband, **King Henry VI**, at Titchfield Abbey. There is still a bridge nearby called Anjou Bridge, perhaps built for the wedding.

Henry Adams came as a shipbuilder to Buckler's Hard in 1745, married a local girl and stayed. In a long career he built fifty-two ships for the Admiralty there. His life spanned the golden age of Hampshire shipbuilding: he was born in 1713 and died in 1805 aged 92. He made some of the greatest ships of Nelson's era, including HMS *Agamemnon* and HMS *Swiftsure*. You can still see his house at Buckler's Hard. He had it built partly to provide spectators with a good viewing station for his ship launches. He is buried in Beaulieu Church.

Henry Cook was aged only 19 when he swung from the hangman's noose for his part in the Swing Riots of 1830; violent action from men demanding better pay and conditions for farmworkers. Those arrested in Hampshire appeared before a government-appointed special commission in Winchester. Henry had wielded a sledgehammer at William Baring and knocked off his hat in one of the fracas in Micheldever, and he had been charged with attempted murder. Many death sentences were commuted to transportation but two Hampshire men, including young Henry, were hanged. To add to the misery of all the other convicted men, they were made to watch.

'Brusher' or **Harry Mills,** known as a New Forest folk hero, was a snake catcher in the late 1800s. He moved into an old charcoal burner's hut near Brockenhurst in his 40s and caught snakes for a living. He is said to have caught over 30,000 in his career, with a forked stick and a sack, sending some to London Zoo for the birds of prey and some to make into ointment to treat ailments. He became a tourist attraction at the local fairs. He lived contentedly in his mud hut until it was vandalised. Distraught, he moved into an outbuilding of the Railway Inn in Brockenhurst. He died not long after, in 1905, and is buried in St Nicholas's Church, where local people paid for a marble headstone. He is said to have been given the 'Brusher' nickname for sweeping the cricket pitch at Balmer Lawn between innings whenever a match was played.

Henry, or **Henri, Portal** was a refugee French Huguenot, who learned the art of papermaking in Stoneham, Southampton. His is truly a rags-to-riches story in two senses of the phrase. In 1712 he set up his own papermaking mill at Bere on the River Test. The pure chalk stream water was perfect for making high-quality paper and also supplied power for the mill. The paper was hardwearing enough to win the contract for making banknotes for the Bank of England in 1724, and by then Portal had opened another mill at Laverstoke. The process of papermaking began with rags cut into strips and beaten to a pulp with hammers powered by a water wheel. It was then put in moulds, pressed, dried, glazed, rollered and trimmed. Henri Portal perfected this method in the 1700s, and by 1962, Portals was providing paper for the banknotes of no fewer than 101 separate governments and banks of issue throughout the five continents, making it the largest banknote paper mill in the world. It made the family one of the major players in the county, with different generations holding such positions as High Sheriff of Hampshire, Justice of the Peace and Deputy Lieutenant of Hampshire. The area around Laverstoke and Overton (where a further larger factory was opened in 1922) serviced the industry, with around 1,550 employees in the 1960s.

A slightly more modern, but very successful, Hampshire 'money' business that doesn't use paper at all is **GoHenry**. Louise Hill from Lymington founded it to provide pre-paid payment cards and an app (with parental controls) for children aged 6 to 18, hoping to bring an understanding of money to the first generation of 'cashless natives'. GoHenry now has over 1.5 million customers in the UK and America.

JULIETTE, JAMES AND TWO JOHNS

Juliette de Bairacli-Levy was a pioneer of holistic animal care and lived for three years with her two small children in a tiny cottage at Abbots Well, near Frogham, in the New Forest. She is reported to have cured many animals by herbal methods. She developed her own brand of herbal pet products and published several herbal handbooks. She is credited with curing a herd of 3,000 sheep condemned by black scour in Yorkshire during the Second World War by feeding them green herbs, milk and molasses. Her book *Wanderers of the New Forest* (1958) described a simple but disappearing way of life. Juliette was friends with the gypsies of the New Forest and wrote about them in the book, too.

John Pounds was a man of the people of Portsmouth and founded one of the first ragged schools for the very poorest children in Old Portsmouth. Pounds was apprenticed to a shipwright but was crippled for life after falling into a dry dock. He became a shoemaker and by 1803 had his own shop in St Mary Street, Portsmouth, a tiny house where he also kept guinea pigs, magpies, finches and cats. In 1818 he began teaching poor children reading, writing, and arithmetic without charging fees. He spent time on the streets and quays of Portsmouth making contact and even bribing them to come with the offer of baked potatoes. Later he also gave lessons in cooking, carpentry and shoemaking, and took the students up to Portsdown Hill on hot days. He must have improved the lives of many in this tough area and said of his charges, 'One or two of 'em were transported, but none o' mine was ever hanged.' Pounds died in 1839, apparently, like one of his pet birds, falling off its perch – he simply keeled over in a friend's hallway. His model inspired many other ragged schools.

John Marshall of Seacourt House, South Hayling on Hayling Island, set up the first anti-mosquito scheme in Britain, the Hayling Mosquito Control. At the time in 1921, the island was infested with mosquitoes. He set up an eleven-room laboratory in the grounds of his house and many visitors from all over the world came to see him and his work. His work means that the saltwater mosquito now no longer bothers the inhabitants of the island. The last real tennis court was also built by him in 1910–11 (still going today). He was a great enthusiast of the sport and even held the World Open Real Tennis Tournament.

The ultimate saver of drenched people is the umbrella, popularised in England by James Hanway of Portsmouth, born in 1712. An innovation from France, carrying an umbrella was vilified in England as effeminate, weak and above all French! But Hanway didn't care and pushed through the taboo, using his umbrella and often attracting abuse in the street. On one occasion, a hansom cab driver even tried to run Hanway over with his coach. Hanway reacted by using his umbrella to 'give the man a good thrashing'. After his death, umbrella use rose steadily. He also started a fund for providing greatcoats for the soldiers of the Seven Years' War and championed street paving. This man certainly had his mind on keeping dry!

FOUR PASSIONATE BUT UNFORTUNATE (EXCEPT ONE) MARYS

Many of us are now familiar with a Shaker kitchen – one of simple and clean design. It arose from the style of furniture made by a religious sect called the Shakers, who believed in the simple life. They made many things themselves as they thought it was wrong to work for money and believed in the common ownership of goods. They called themselves the Children of God, but were also called Shakers after the unusual way they worshiped: dancing and shaking with great fervour. Mary

Girling led the sect in Hordle near the New Forest and they lived at what is now Hordle Grange, until they were evicted and went to live in tents in the near village of Tiptoe. Although Girling believed she was immortal, she did in fact die in 1886 and is buried at Hordle churchyard, in an unmarked grave along with other members of her sect.

Mary Collier was one of the first published working-class female writers. She was born into poverty around 1690 and forced to find work as a washer woman in Petersfield when her father died. In 1730 Stephen Duck wrote an attack on the 'indolence and laziness' of countrywomen. Mary was furious and channelled her anger into a reply. However, it was nine years before it was published as *The Woman's Labour: An Epistle to Mr Stephen Duck*. She did not profit from her writing and continued to work as a washer woman until she was 63, when she moved to Alton to run a farm. She died in a tiny attic room in Alton, poor and alone.

Queen Mary I and Philip of Spain (later King of Spain) were married in 1554 in Winchester Cathedral by Bishop Stephen Gardiner and had their wedding feast at Wolvesey Palace. After arriving in Southampton, Philip finally met Queen Mary on the evening of 23 July in the bishop's gardens before their marriage the next day. She was eleven years his senior, at 38. The records of the royal wardrobe tell us that the dress was in the French style made of 'rich tissue with a border and wide sleeves, embroidered upon purple satin, set with pearls of our store, line with purple taffeta'. The kirtle

The chair, used by Queen Mary Tudor at her wedding to Prince Philip of Spain in 1554, is kept at Winchester Cathedral.

was of white satin enriched with silver and a train. A replica of the dress was made for the 450th anniversary of the wedding in 2004. In thanks for hosting her wedding at such great expense, the city of Winchester was given the land that is now Abbey Gardens and the City Mill. The cathedral still has her wedding chair and uses the hooks in the nave pillars that were used for her wedding tapestries for modern decorative banners.

Mary Elizabeth Braddon was a prolific writer in the mid-1800s and created the new school of 'sensationalist' writing. Her most famous book was *Lady Audley's Secret*. With her husband, she built a house at Bank near Lyndhurst as a country retreat. She was so famous at the time that her holidays there were usually announced in the papers and her house was a stop on charabanc tours of the New Forest. Her follow-up novel, *Henry Dunbar: The Story of an Outcast*, is set in Basingstoke, Winchester and Southampton, and features a murder in Winchester's water meadows.

LIBERTY-LOVING LUCIA, LAURA AND LICORICIA

Lady Laura Ridding, wife of George Ridding, Headmaster of Winchester College and resident of Wonston later in life, was an author and suffragist, playing a key role in the National Union of Women Workers. One of her most famous works was a response to a speech made by Lord Curzon of Kedleston on 18 May 1909 at the meeting of the Men's League for Opposing Woman Suffrage. In the speech he had said there were 'fifteen sound, valid and incontrovertible arguments against the Grant of Female Suffrage'. He argued that the vote, if given, would 'lead women away from their maternal duty, bring disharmony to the home and result in further demands being made'. In response to these arguments, Lady Laura wrote her own article. One by one, Lord Curzon's fifteen arguments meet their end – for example by 'dying of inconsistency' or being 'squashed flat by progress', until the final paragraph in which it is stated:

> No valid argument will win of all the great fifteen
> They will have vanished into dust as if they'd never been.

Lucia Foster Welch lived in Southampton in the early part of the twentieth century and was actively involved in the suffragette movement, hosting a visit from Emmeline Pankhurst in 1911. She took her chance in 1918 during the First World War and was co-opted as the first female town councillor. She was then able to defend her seat in an election and in 1927 became the first female Mayor of Southampton.

Licoricia had a unique name and an unusual life. She lived in Winchester's Jewish community in the 1200s and was one of its most successful (but not only) businesswomen. She worked as a money lender to many influential people, including King Henry III. She married twice, had at least four children and had a stone-built house on Jewry Street. The death duties she was forced to pay to the king after her very wealthy second husband, David of Oxford, died probably paid for the great shrine of Edward the Confessor in Westminster Abbey (although she negotiated the amount down considerably). Licoricia was very clever, probably speaking several languages. She was clearly diplomatic and eloquent, moving between the royal court at Winchester Castle and her own Jewish community based around the Jewry Street area. But these were dangerous times for Jewish people. Although she lived through a massacre of Jews when Simon de Montfort came through Winchester during the Barons' War of 1265, her own son was hanged for financial misdealing during the coin-clipping pogrom of 1278–79, and she herself was found murdered in her Jewry Street home along with her Christian maid in 1277. She was so famous that the news was carried all through Europe. A statue of her stands in Jewry Street, Winchester.

8

NATURE

… the sight of a chalk stream running between the meadows, slow but not sluggish, and clear to the pebbles between the white patches of water crowfoot, is not to be neglected among the good things of Wessex.

Geoffrey Grigson in *About Britain*
No. 2 Wessex, 1951

WAITING PATIENTLY, 'OBSERVING NARROWLY' AND 'STUDYING TO BE QUIET': NATURALISTS OF HAMPSHIRE

Eric Ashby (1918–2003) was one of the first wildlife filmmakers. He shot his films in the New Forest with extraordinary patience and was one of the first to show wild animals behaving naturally. It took four years to get enough footage for forty-five minutes of *The Unknown Forest* (1961). He was a strong conservationist and spoke out about hunting and protecting badgers. His home near Linwood was home to many rescued foxes.

Izaak Walton published *The Compleat Angler* in 1653 and it has gone through more than 500 editions since. Ostensibly about fishing, it's actually a dialogue on the beauty of enjoying pastoral life and outdoor recreation. Born in Stafford, Izaak Walton spent his final years in Winchester as steward to Bishop Morley from 1660. He visited his son-in-law at Droxford often and he no doubt fished in the River Meon, which he considered to be the best river in England for trout. East Meon has a pub named in his honour, while the Fisherman Apostles chapel in Winchester

Being a Difcourfe of

FISH and FISHING,

Not unworthy the perufal of moft *Anglers.*

Simon Peter *faid, I go a* fifhing : *and they faid, We alfo wil go with thee.* John 21.3.

London, Printed by *T. Maxey* for RICH. MARRIOT, in S. *Dunftans* Church-yard Fleetftreet, 1653.

The frontispiece to The Compleat Angler *by Izaak Walton (although published anonymously) in 1653.*

Cathedral, his final resting place, has a memorial window funded by 'followers of the Gentle Art' (fishing) and an altar inspired by *The Compleat Angler*'s depiction of nature in vegetation and fish. If you look closely you can also find him as a figure on the cathedral's Great Screen and in the embroidered cushions of the cathedral. His famous yet enigmatic instruction to us to 'study to be quiet' might be explained by a further quotation from him: 'Rivers and the inhabitants of the watery elements are made for wise men to contemplate and for fools to pass by without consideration.'

There have been many beekeepers in Hampshire over the centuries, not least in its monasteries. However, Wootten St Lawrence was home to a beekeeper and rector for forty-seven years, Rev. Charles Butler. He was author of one of the seminal works on bees, *The Feminine Monarchie*, in the early 1600s. In it he refuted the common myth that there was a king bee and instead talked about the queen bee and identified worker bees as female and without a sting. He argued that each hive has its own scent and that 'the work of the little Bee is so great and wonderful, so comely for order and beauty, so excellent for Art and wisdom; & so full of pleasure and profit; that the contemplation thereof may well beseeme an ingenious nature'. Incredibly, the book includes a musical score based on the sounds of a bee swarm, a so-called 'bees madrigal' (Butler was musically trained and a chorister at Magdalen College, Oxford)!

John Goodyer, born in Alton in 1592, was a noted botanist of the seventeenth century. He lived in a time of the first botanic gardens and of exploration, and he added many plants to the British flora. He had the reputation of being one of the most knowledgeable herbalists in England. He classified elm trees and found one endemic to Hampshire (Goodyer's elm, no longer existing) and introduced the Jerusalem artichoke as a culinary vegetable. He has a memorial window at Buriton but one of his greatest legacies was the money he left as a charity in his will, which went towards helping many poor people of Petersfield and apprenticing many young people. It still exists today.

William Curtis (1746–99) lived in Alton and was a pre-eminent botanist of his day. He published *The Botanical Magazine, or Flower Garden Displayed*, a very successful magazine with a circulation of 3,000. It made his fortune and he set up botanical gardens in Bermondsey, Lambeth and Brompton.

Gilbert White (1720–93) was a ground-breaking, if quiet and humble, naturalist and ecologist. His dispassionate but full recordings of living nature (not dead specimens) around Selborne in his most famous book, *The Natural History and Antiquities of Selborne*, provide a special picture of Hampshire and indeed Britain. The book has appealed to generations since and has never been out of print. Indeed, it is said to be the most printed book after the Bible, Shakespeare's works and *A Pilgrim's Progress*. He identified new bird species (wood warbler, chiffchaff and willow warbler) from their song alone; that the owl's hoot was in B flat; and the importance of earthworms to the 'interlinking of all nature', among other things. His method involved 'observing narrowly' and then carefully recording what he observed. His observations of nature, weather and his garden are so particular to Selborne and yet his approach had such importance for nature studies and ecology all over the world. Richard Mabey, naturalist and his biographer, said, 'Gilbert White's book, more than any other, has shaped our everyday view of the relations between humans and nature.' He was admired by Charles Darwin, Edward Thomas and David Attenborough, among many others. Inside Selborne Church is a picture of St Francis of Assisi with the sixty-four types of birds White mentions in his great book. His house and restored garden in Selborne, The Wakes, is open as a museum.

Chris Packham is a famous wildlife TV presenter, photographer and activist, particularly known for *The Really Wild Show* and *Springwatch*. He was born and grew up in

Southampton. Exploring nature in this county as a boy led to his subsequent career and passionate defence of wildlife. He is especially connected to Hampshire, living in the county in the New Forest and being president of the Hawk Conservancy Trust, Hampshire Ornithological Society, Southampton Natural History Society, as well as many national wildlife organisations. In 2011 he was awarded the Dilys Breese medal by the British Trust for Ornithology, for 'outstanding work in promoting science to new audiences'.

BIRD WATCHERS

Anthony Collett (1877–1929) was a nature writer and a plot of land in Woolton Hill, donated as a wildlife reserve and bird sanctuary by his friend Sir Kenneth Swan, is dedicated to him. Collett's books include *The English Year*, *The Changing Face of England* (much quoted by W.H. Auden in his poems) and *The Heart of a Bird*.

James Aldred is an Emmy-winning wildlife filmmaker, but his latest project is a little closer to home and is based on a summer watching goshawks and their chicks in the New Forest during the pandemic lockdown in 2020. His book *Goshawk Summer* documents the family.

John Latham may not be as famous a name as Gilbert White, as eighteenth-century naturalists go, but he too produced wonderful works of ornithology, antiquarianism and the study of nature in the late 1700s and early 1800s. He latterly lived in Romsey and Winchester and published his ten-volume *A General History of Birds*, covering 3,000 species. Sadly, he took his own life in 1822 before he saw the last volumes published. His daughter, Ann, was also a talented nature illustrator and made many drawings herself for the volumes.

ALL CREATURES GREAT ...

The New Forest is a unique place to find wildlife due to its patchwork of wet and dry heaths, bogs, ancient pasture woodland, farmland, coniferous plantations, acid grasslands and coast.

The New Forest has large populations of deer, as one would expect, given it started life as a hunting ground for the Norman kings:

- Around 1,300 fallow deer, which is the one William the Conqueror and his family will have hunted. Hunting it was outlawed in 1997.
- Red deer are native and number around ninety in the west part of the New Forest.
- Roe deer, another native, number around 350–400.
- Sika deer, imported from East Asia by the Beaulieu Estate in 1900, number around 100 in the east of the forest.

New Forest ponies are not wild but are left to graze around the forest as a right to common pasture attached to properties there. The ponies are all branded with their owner's mark but are handled very infrequently, so are semi-feral. The New Forest is a females-only preserve – when it comes to ponies anyway. Stallions are only released for a limited period between May and June each year.

The New Forest pony is a recognised breed, however, with special characteristics. It can be no taller than 14.2 hands (or 1.44m) and has elements of Welsh, Thoroughbred, Arab and Hackney, and pony bloodlines of Fell, Dales, Highlands, Dartmoor and Exmoor. This has produced a breed that is distinguished by its versatility, intelligence and friendliness. According to the New Forest Pony Breeding Society, 'New Forest ponies can be any colour except piebald, skewbald, spotted or blue-eyed cream.' Five agisters, employed for each of five forest districts, manage the stock of animals and the yearly 'drifts', where animals are driven into pounds for worming, counting, branding, tail marking and selling.

Rare reptiles in the New Forest include the sand lizard, which was reintroduced in the 1980s, and the smooth snake, which likes to eat sand lizards!

The pine marten was once thought extinct in England. However, the weasel-like mammal has since made an appearance in several areas including the New Forest, its only home in the southern-central area of England.

AND SMALL ...

The New Forest is home to three incredibly rare bats. The barbastrelle, Bechstein's – sometimes called 'the rarest mammal in Europe', but with four known breeding sites in the New Forest – and the greater horseshoe, one of our largest but rarest bats.

The New Forest is also a stronghold for dragonflies and damselflies. Alongside many more common ones in its watery areas, there are rarer ones to spot. The small red damselfly likes to breed in unshaded, shallow, acidic water – tiny pools or even wheel ruts – and the extremely rare southern damselfly.

Beetle species you might not see anywhere else include: the brown diving beetle; the flame-shouldered blister beetle (incidentally, if you see one of these you should photograph it and report it to Buglife, it is so rare), which is a parasite on the hairy-footed flower bee; the very rare noble chafer, a beautiful green-glowing species found near Brockenhurst and Lymington (another one to record if seen, and send a photo to the People's Trust for Endangered Species); also the extremely rare scarlet malachite, found only in North and South Gorley and Minstead, usually near thatched houses; and the scarce stag beetle, whose antlers, although harmless to humans, are used to fight other males at mating time, like deer do.

Rare butterflies can be seen in the New Forest, again thanks to the heathland plants and special conservation practices such as coppicing. These include the pearl bordered and small pearl bordered fritillary, silver-studded blue and white admiral. Hampshire has also become a stronghold for the declining Duke of Burgundy butterfly and the marsh fritillary thanks to Butterfly Conservation.

The New Forest has 1,460 species of moth, 58 per cent of Britain's total, so is a top area for lepidopterists. Rare moths include Clifden nonpareil, dark crimson underwing and light crimson underwing, and the goat moth (whose larvae burrow into trees and when they exit the larval chamber is said to smell 'goat-like').

EXTREME WEATHER EVENTS IN HAMPSHIRE

Terrible weather of 1140 that cast Henri de Blois, Bishop of Winchester, and/or his brother King Stephen ashore at the place that became Gosport is the supposed origin of the name Gosport or God's Port. However, it seems the first reference to this origin story was in 1811 and it has since been amplified by the design of the borough crest in 1922.

The winter of 1684 was perhaps the coldest in Hampshire history. Southampton Water froze over from bank to bank. Miniature icebergs massed in the Dover Strait, closing Southampton port for several days. Huge snow drifts proved lethal to travellers.

In 1703, on 26 November, there was the Great Storm, as it was known. After an extreme hurricane through the night, Hampshire woke to find buildings in ruins and thousands of trees strewn about (including the great oak on Selborne Plestor). Over 400 windmills were smashed.

Gilbert White records 1776 as a bitter year. On 31 January he recorded -18°C just before sunrise. The Itchen, Test and Hamble were frozen over and 'in the day, wind was so keen that persons of robust constitutions could scarcely endure to face it … By the time the thaw came in early February, the thrushes and blackbirds were mostly destroyed.'

On 18 January 1881 a huge snowstorm rolled in. There was almost a total suspension of business in Portsmouth and Southampton. The borough engineer of Portsmouth estimated that 11 million cubic metres of snow fell on the town. The sea froze in temperatures of -12°C, including even the Inner Dock at Southampton.

Another bad snowstorm, and an unexpected one for late April, occurred in 1908. Snow began to fall at 4 a.m. on Saturday, 25 April and caused high snowdrifts, closed roads and non-delivery of provisions. Cancelling of the Alton fair followed, many new lambs died and the fruit harvest was destroyed. In Winchester the aviary in Abbey Gardens was destroyed and 'the whole fell with a great noise. Fortunately the birds escaped unhurt and only a couple of doves were killed but it was curious to see the goldfinches gathered at one end of the aviary in fright of the iron wreckage.' Warm weather returned by Sunday and by Monday there was barely any remnant of the storm.

There was a great drought in 1921, when the rainfall was less than would fall in Alice Springs in the Australian desert.

The winter of 1947 was very bitter and harsh and the suffering was added to by the post-war shortages. Thousands of workers were unemployed due to power cuts; rations were reduced, fuel ran low and shipping in the Channel was stopped by persistent blizzards, which added to the food shortages. In Aldershot, despite no electricity, 200 men took part in the Hampshire Military District cross-country run – in a snowstorm! Many schools closed and the hills, including Portsdown Hill, filled up with young tobogganists. The cold and coal shortages didn't let up until March 1947 and were followed by great floods caused by the thaw.

In 1959 there was an incredibly hot summer, almost unbroken from 5 July to October. On 7 and 8 July calls to the fire service broke previous records for a single day, with 124 and 141 respectively. People flocked to the New Forest in the summer weather and 104 accidents with animals were recorded. Hotels were packed and many slept on the beach. Household water supplies ran low but the chalk rivers were never in danger of drying up and were a boon to the county.

The harsh winter of 1963 led to pack ice extending well out into the Solent. Many roads were blocked and at the County Surveyor's Department in Winchester they even ran out of red pins to show the location of blockages! Apparently, though, Hampshire's roads were better than other southern counties due to the policy of gritting roads before the first snowfall. Hampshire employed 500 men, 234 snow ploughs and fifty bulldozers to deal with the snow. The New Forest Association and the RSPCA began a huge effort to feed the New Forest ponies with bales of hay.

Hampshire had white Christmases in the following years: 1906 (beginning 10 p.m. Christmas night), 1927, 1938, 1956, 1962 (actually snow began on Boxing Day after a very cold Christmas Day) and 1981.

In the hot summer of 1976, fires broke out all over Hampshire. At an Army show at Rushmoor Arena, 1,139 heatstroke casualties were treated. More unusually, adders, basking in the heat more than usual, became a problem. A huge fire at Matchams in the New Forest travelled at 40mph: every fireman in Hampshire was summoned; residents of a hospital at Ringwood had to be evacuated; and trains were stopped as embankments burnt. Ironically, Hampshire also suffered floods as water mains pipes fractured as the ground contracted!

The Great Storm of 16 October 1987 hit Hampshire at 2 a.m. With wind speeds in excess of 100mph, roof tiles flew around like frisbies and electricity lines and most phone lines were out.

At Portsmouth Naval Base, boats were pulled out to sea. A block of flats partially collapsed at Barton-on-Sea, there were several fatalities from falling trees and the big wheel at Hayling Island came down.

Just three years later, on 25 January 1990, another huge storm hit, but this time it was at least predicted. The casualty list was high though, with six fatalities in the county. At Lasham Airfield, near Alton, thirty gliders were hurled across fields and roads. It was believed that Hampshire lost 500,000 trees, including 60,000 in the New Forest. Many had been weakened first by the 1987 storm and now came down. This included Morestead Down near Twyford, where hundreds fell, and the Selborne Yew, finally felled after living for between 1,200 and 1,400 years, revealing the bones of an ancient burial. Hampshire Police had the busiest day they had ever known, with 2,334 incidents reported.

On 20 October 2013, at least 100 properties on Hayling Island were damaged when it was hit by a tornado. No injuries were reported.

The weather on each St Swithun's Day, 15 July, it is said, predicts the next forty days of weather, whether fair or foul. It doesn't always work, however; the longest spell of consecutive wet days after 15 July was in 1939, when apparently 15 July itself was completely dry! Conversely, in 1913 there was a rainstorm lasting fifteen hours on 15 July that was followed by mainly dry weather.

ANCIENT TREES

Yews thrive on chalk downland and Hampshire has a large number of ancient examples. Yews are the longest-lived tree by far, many ancient ones having a 'birthday' stretching back millennia. Yews have a spiritual significance and have often been preserved in churchyards.

The yew tree at Farringdon churchyard is certified as over 3,000 years old and measures 9.27m girth at its narrowest point. It is considered by arboriculturists to be one of the ten most important trees in the country. There is a second one nearby in the churchyard, which is merely half the age, 1,500 years old.

West Tisted, near Bramdean, has a tiny hidden church, with beautiful Saxon and Norman stonework, but also an ancient yew said be to over 1,500 years old. The hollow trunk can fit a (small) person inside!

At Bentley, near Farnham, there is an incredible yew avenue in the churchyard with a yew branch canopy overhead. Although the trees are not ancient, the effect is dramatic.

The yew tree in the churchyard at Twyford is 650 years old and said to be the oldest clipped one in the country. It is clipped into a sort of hat shape.

St Mary's churchyard in South Hayling has an ancient yew of 9m girth.

Other ancient yews in Hampshire churchyards include those at: Bedhampton, Brockenhurst, Fareham, Greatham, Hurstbourne Priors, Long Sutton, Priors Dean, Tangley, Boarhunt, Corhampton, Hambledon, Itchen Abbas, Newton Valence, St Mary Bourne, Steep, Warblington, Woodcott, Breamore, Durley, Froxfield Green, Hawkley, Lockerley, Owslebury, Selborne and Steventon.

The New Forest National Park has the highest concentration of ancient trees anywhere in Western Europe, around 1,000.

The largest and oldest oak tree in Hampshire is next to the River Test at Mottisfont, the Oakley Oak, which is between 800 and 1,100 years old.

The Naked Man is a 6ft-high stump of an aged oak tree on the old Lymington to Ringwood road near Wilverley Post and it is said the hanging of smugglers took place there.

The Knightwood Oak, in the New Forest, south of Bolderwood Ornamental Drive, is a 500-year-old pollarded oak. The eighteen trees around it in the Monarchs Grove represent all the visits by reigning monarchs to the New Forest, plus one planted by Queen Elizabeth II in 1979 to mark the ninth centenary of the forest.

There is a very unusual couple of trees near the grove, where an oak and a beech have intertwined and in fact united in a process called 'inosculation'. It is a very rare phenomenon in different species of trees.

The Eagle Oak in Knightwood Enclosure is so named because it is said to be the spot where the last white eagle was shot in 1810.

The Gospel Oak in Hampage Wood is so called because it is said to be the first place the gospel was preached in days immemorial. Lying on the parish boundary, it is also said that 'a gospel was wont to be said there in the perambulation week between the lordships of Cheriton and Ovington'.

The Gospel Oak, Hampage Wood, as portrayed in Duthy's Sketches of Hampshire *(1839).*

Undersley Wood, a small area of woodland off the Lyndhurst road next to the Lucy Hill car park, has a number of beautiful ancient oak trees, including the Undersley Oak.

Other notable oaks include the Moyles Court Oak of 7m girth; the Adam Oak, in a Minstead hedge at 7.3m; and the Withybed Oak (5.9m) and Spreading Oak (5.6m) close to each other, near Lucas Castle.

The Rhinefield Ornamental Drive, near Brockenhurst, was planted in 1859 and contains four trees that are the tallest of their species in Great Britain – a redwood, black spruce, red spruce and Spanish fir. The tallest of them all is a Wellingtonia that reaches over 50m.

Beech trees do not live as long, being susceptible to fungi and drought, and can be considered ancient from 225 years old. There are notable examples at Queen Bower, near Brockenhurst (7.3m girth), and Knowles, near Acres Down (7.3m). The largest unpollarded beech tree is at Burley Old Inclosure at 6.7m girth. Mark Ash Wood, Bratley Wood and Ashurst Wood are other places to spot old, large, pollarded beech trees.

A huge horse chestnut can be found by the Bourne rivulet at Hurstbourne Priors. It measures 7.03m girth and was the champion tree of its type until 2014, when another was found to be bigger. It is also one of the tallest and has been called, by tree expert Alan Mitchell, the finest sweet chestnut all round in the country.

Britain's widest pear tree, espaliered, is at Houghton Lodge and measures 16.33m wide.

Although Portsmouth has one of the lowest numbers of trees of any British city, Southsea Common hosts an unusual collection of mature elm trees, believed to be the oldest and largest surviving in Hampshire. They have escaped Dutch elm disease owing to their isolation. Southsea Common is also host to several fruiting Canary Island date palms.

HAMPSHIRE ROSES

The county flower is the Hampshire rose, essentially a simple dog rose, similar to the Tudor rose.

The Minden rose is the emblem of the Hampshire Regiment (now part of the Princess of Wales's Royal Regiment) and comes from the famous battle they fought in 1759 during the Seven Years' War. It was a great victory against superior numbers and the Battle of Minden was placed in the colours of the regiment. The Minden rose was picked as the infantrymen returned from battle. Today, small roses are worn in the headdresses of the regiment on Minden Day, 1 August. A memorial garden to soldiers of the Hampshire Regiment is at their museum on Southgate Street, Winchester, and is full of rose beds.

Mottisfont, near Stockbridge, is a stately home now owned by the National Trust and houses in its walled garden one of the most famous rose gardens in the country, including the national collection of pre-1900 old-fashioned roses, over 500 of them. These roses have one spectacular flowering period in early summer with incredible scent to boot. Mottisfont also serves Hampshire-made Jude's ice cream in rose flavour!

There are roses to buy for your garden with a Hampshire connection:

- Winchester Cathedral is an English shrub rose, with loose white petals, that flowers throughout the summer.
- Hampshire is a small ground cover rose with bright scarlet single flowers.
- Charlie's rose is a hybrid tea rose in cherry pink/red and is named after Hampshire TV gardener Charlie Dimmock.

9

BUILT IN HAMPSHIRE

FOLLIES, FAKES AND FOUR-FOOTED FRIENDS

On the top of Farley Mount, to the west of Winchester, stands a huge pyramid monument dedicated to 'Beware Chalkpit'. This is the name of a horse. The owner, Paulet St John (1704–80) of Farley Chamberlayne, was out hunting in 1733 when he and his horse leapt into a chalk pit 25ft deep. They both survived and the following year the horse, under the name Beware Chalkpit, ridden by its owner, competed at the Hunters Plate race at Winchester Racecourse and won.

There is a stone circle off the A272, near Bramdean, which could be mistaken for a prehistoric place of ritual. However, it was actually created by Colonel Greenwood (see Men of the Trees and Green Men in Chapter 1, What is Hampshire?) around 1845 as a memorial to one of his favourite horses. Across the road, a second monument with a mound of flints and a headstone records a second horse burial by Colonel Richard Meinertzhagen of his horse Melksham, who he buried where he fell in 1910.

If you visit Alresford and walk along the River Alre, you will see a plaque dedicated to a Hambone Junior. This is the name of a dog. It was the devoted mascot of the 47th Infantry Regiment, 9th Division of the US Army. Hambone was a scruffy brown and white terrier and he 'helped' the unit, which specialised in amphibious landings, to train for D-Day. Sadly, he was run over, as the soldiers mobilised, by a 'deuce-and-a-half' (a 2½-ton truck). They marched down to Southampton in June 1944 with a replacement pup, Spider. Hambone Junior's burial was marked by a wooden cross, then a stone plaque, unveiled by the American Consul in Southampton in 1962.

Why do you see pigs all over the top of Winchester's High Street? Because that is the home of Hampshire County Council and the symbol of Hampshire is the Hampshire Hog. Stand at the Westgate and see if you can see three. A fourth one is inside the offices, carved by Arts and Crafts artist Eric Gill.

Massey's Folly in Farringdon was built by the rector Thomas Massey and took thirty years to complete (1870–1900) by himself, with the occasional help of a bricklayer. It is a strange, eccentric building, with seventeen bedrooms, two towers, unusual rounded gables and many terracotta panels, the whole looking like something M.C. Esher would draw.

Luttrell's Tower, near Calshot, has three storeys with a six-storey staircase tower. It was built in 1780 for Temple Simon Luttrell, an MP who was also rumoured to be involved in smuggling operations, and is now a holiday home. It can't be proven, but the fact that the tower has a commanding view of the area, including inland and the coast, and a tunnel that runs from the beach to the tower, seems suspicious.

EIGHT ISOLATED OCTAGONS

Micheldever Church has an unconventional octagonal nave, built in 1808–09 by George Dance junior. It sits next to a sixteenth-century tower.

Odiham Castle's keep, built for King John in 1207–14, is octagonal. There is only one other in the country (in Chilham, Kent).

The remains of Warblington Castle. Print by Ruth Ander.

Warblington used to have a huge castle. Thanks to the Civil War it is no more, and most of the stones apparently ended up in Portsmouth buildings. One tall, slender, octagonal tower remains, like Rapunzel's tower and is an easily spotted landmark on the horizon near Havant.

Winchester's Buttercross, the ancient market cross and meeting place, dates from the 1400s, is one of the tallest in the country at 13.2m and is one of the best-loved places in Winchester. The base is made of five octagonal steps. In 1770 the Pavement Commissioners of Winchester were unaware of this passionate feeling and attempted to sell it to Mr Dummer, gentleman of Cranbury Park. He wished it to adorn his estate as a Gothic folly, as was the fashion of the time. When his workmen came to remove it, they were faced with a small riot of townspeople. The workmen were forced back, the deal had to be undone and Mr Dummer had to be content with a lath and plaster version, which stood for sixty years or so.

A very unusual folly is Peterson's folly or Sway tower, which features fourteen storeys and 60m of unreinforced concrete (the first and tallest building in Britain to use this material) with an octagonal spiral staircase tower (nearly 400 steps) on the side to reach them all. It was built by Andrew Peterson in 1885 after his return from India as the centrepiece to his Hampshire estate, and allegedly after a seance in which he spoke to Sir Christopher Wren! He also wanted to prove concrete's versatility.

At the ruined Basing House there are two octagonal banqueting houses or 'turrets' in the wall of the Tudor garden, later turned into dovecotes. It is thought King Henry VIII walked in this garden with Anne Boleyn in 1535.

New Milton has an octagonal water tower of around 1900 that one could mistake for a castle, with windows and battlements.

All that remains of George Staunton's regency house at Leigh Park near Havant is the roofless, octagonal, Gothic library, which he used to hold his huge collection of Chinese books. He had lived in China, was one of the earliest Englishmen to speak Mandarin and his garden was used to show off his Sinophile leanings. Only a few remain of the garden features and follies that he and his predecessor, William Garrett, built. They include the Shell House, which was built in 1828 and constructed of Hampshire flints and seashells gathered on Hayling Island. Plaques inside commemorate the Staunton family and it used to contain such exotic curiosities as a stuffed crocodile, sea hedgehog, toucan's bill, a nautilus shell, specimens of lava, 'Wedgewood's designs', archaeological finds such as a Roman key and many types of unusual minerals and stones. Other garden buildings included a classical temple with twenty-four busts, a Chinese bridge, a hermitage, an Indian temple, a Swiss house, a cone house decorated with fir cones, a lookout, a cross-shaped house, the Beacon (or Ionic temple), a 15m-high obelisk, an election column recording George Staunton's Parliamentary election victories and losses, a man-made lake with three islands

– one with a Chinese fort built on it and one with a cottage – a Turkish summerhouse and a statue of Diana.

UNUSUAL BUILDINGS

Alresford has a restored Eel House, used to trap eels for the family at Arlebury Park House and for London's Billingsgate market. The incredible life cycle of the eels sees them travel on dark, moonless nights in the autumn, down the rivers Alre and Itchen to the English Channel, across the Atlantic, where they spawn in the Sargasso Sea. Unless they're caught in the eel house first.

The dovecote in the churchyard at Broughton is a rare survivor of the many originally around the county and was built to house 483 pairs of pigeons. It also has a rare rotating ladder.

The Grange, Northington, is a grand former house but now stands empty. It is also a house in the Greek Revival style, one of the finest examples in Europe, in fact; a magnificent and slightly eerie edifice. Looking like it was taken from Athens and plonked in the Hampshire countryside, it was in fact built around an existing house between 1809 and 1816 by architect William Watkins for its owner, Henry Drummond. It has survived the Army being stationed there in the Second World War and later plans for demolition by dynamite, and is now owned by English Heritage and hosts an annual opera festival.

There is an old pest house, in Ramsdean Road, Stroud, built in 1703 to house victims of infectious diseases including plague and smallpox. Many villages and towns had one, but here is a surviving example. It is now Mount Pleasant Farm. Another survives at Odiham, behind the church.

John King was a shipwright at Emsworth, known for erecting perhaps the first prefabricated house in 1795 at No. 19 Kings Street, Emsworth. It took sixteen hours to construct after all the wooden pieces and chimneys had been made in his shipyard.

King John's House in Romsey is an unusual example of a hall house from around 1250, one of the few in England to survive without major alteration.

Farley Chamberlayne has an old semaphore telegraph station. Part of the high-speed communications line for the Admiralty between Plymouth and London (taking an average of five minutes to reach London), this one ran telegraph messages between Cheesefoot Head and Sherfield English, via the movement of two mechanical arms.

Crinkle crankle is a type of wall that is found mainly in Hampshire and Suffolk. They look like they sound, a bit like large-scale corrugated cardboard. They are built to catch more sunshine, create warmth and shelter and provide good growing conditions for fruit trees. Some can be seen at Lymington still in Church Lane and School Lane.

Hythe got a very long pier in 1878 (one of the ten longest in the country), which allowed passengers for the ferry to the other side of Southampton Water to alight without getting their feet wet. In 1922 a railway followed to transport them and their baggage to the end of the 640m pier. It used electric engines previously used in a mustard gas factory. It continues to run and is the longest continuously running pier railway in the world.

The Woolhouse in Southampton, near the Watergate, is the only surviving medieval warehouse in the county. It was also used later on as a prison and then by the Moon family for their boat and aircraft building. Edwin Moon built the Moonbeam II plane there in 1910 and this became the first plane to take off at what became Southampton Airport.

Alton war memorial is in an odd format – it resembles a drystone beehive and is based on the monument that was raised over the spot where Captain Scott of the Antarctic was found lying dead.

What seems from afar to be a sort of striped black and white castle on the waterside at Warsash turns out to be the harbour master's office. Another strange, but cheerful, paint choice is the pink ferry shelter, which can be seen a little further along the water. This is highly visible from Hamble on the far side of the River Hamble, from where the ferries, also pink, depart. The ferries have been working on this stretch of water since at least 1493.

MAZES AND MOSAICS

Hampshire has two of only eight remaining turf mizmazes in the country. Labyrinth-like and cut into the turf, they are found only in England, their purpose a mystery. A mizmaze at Breamore House is similar in design to mazes at Chartres Cathedral and Bayeux Abbey, probably medieval but its origins are unknown. There is a second mizmaze on St Catherine's Hill, just outside Winchester. It has been connected to Winchester College, who own the hill and play games there. Some even say it was cut by a boy condemned to spend the holidays on the hill. You can walk it yourself now, as the boys do at the college, where it is called Tolling the Labyrinth.

Itchen Stoke Church was only built in 1866 and was designed with inspiration from Saint Chapelle, Paris, and incorporates a tiled maze in its apse.

If you wander around the Inner Cathedral Close at Winchester you may come across the bookstall in the loggia of the Deanery. Make sure you look at the tiles on the floor and see among them a Roman mosaic. This was found and lifted from nearby Dome Alley and is one of the only Roman mosaics still near its original location and in fact able to be walked on.

The Romans left us a few mosaics in Hampshire. Winchester City Museum has a magnificent mosaic from Sparsholt Villa, lifted with very little damage, as well as parts of others found in Winchester.

There is a hidden angel mosaic in an exterior corner at Mottisfont Abbey, now a National Trust site. It is the work of Boris Anrep, a Russian artist, who visited the house in the 1930s

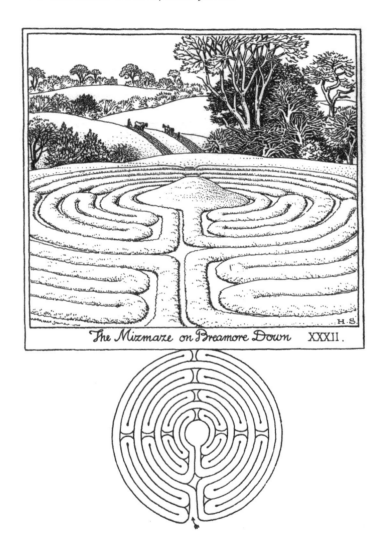

Breamore mizmaze by Heywood Sumner.

and '40s and was a friend and lover of Maud Russell, the owner of the house. It is the guardian angel of the house (formerly an abbey) and Maud wrote in her diary that it was '... a shrine, delicate and mysterious'.

POST OFFICES AND PILLAR BOXES

Milford-on-sea can claim the oldest pillar box in Hampshire, one of the twenty oldest in England, from 1856, although it's possibly moved from elsewhere, as even Milford-on-sea isn't as old as the post box!

Denmead has the second oldest pillar box in Hampshire dating to 1859. It is one of twenty-three surviving National Standard pillar boxes.

There is an extremely rare pillar box on Alresford Road, Winchester, just outside the Golden Lion pub. It dates from King Edward VIII's reign, the king who abdicated within a few months of inheriting the crown in 1936. It follows that only a very few post boxes were manufactured during his reign.

Kings Worthy has a very old post office, once claimed to be the first in the country. Opened in 1845, with a Noah Vincent as postmaster, it is certainly one of the very earliest. The old post office remained in the same building until 1966, though is now a private house on London Road.

PUBS WITH STORIES

The Flying Bull at Rake, on the A3, not only has an unusual name (perhaps derived from two famous coaches that used the A3 road, the Fly and the Bull) but can also claim to be cut in half by the county boundary, being partly in Hampshire and partly in West Sussex. Its Two Counties bar and notice from the ceiling show this. It was also the scene of a shootout in 1786. Murderers of an unknown sailor in Hindhead had fled here and were apprehended and captured at the inn, but not before trying to shoot their way out.

The Royal Oak in Winchester claims to be the oldest bar in England – it certainly has a chequered history and a cellar bar with Anglo-Saxon walls. The Red Lion in Chalton also has a claim to being the oldest pub, with the building dating back to the 1100s.

The Red Lion in Southampton is said to be where three noblemen, Richard, Earl of Cambridge, Sir Thomas Grey of Heton and Lord Scrope of Masham, were tried for treason. They had plotted to assassinate King Henry V and replace him with Edmund Mortimer, Earl of March. They were tried in the half-timbered 'Trial Room', found guilty and executed at Bargate.

The Old Bat and Ball, Cranfield, near Hambledon, is known as the cradle of cricket, as it borders the cricket ground of Broadhalfpenny Down, Hambledon Cricket Club's ground, and was owned by the captain of the team in the mid-1700s.

The Golden Lion at Southwick became an unofficial officers' mess in the run-up to D-Day and served the likes of Generals Eisenhower (who drank half pints of bitter) and Montgomery (who drank only grapefruit juice).

BEAUTIFUL AND INTERESTING HAMPSHIRE CHURCHES

On Bramdean Common can be found, nearly hidden by trees, a tin tabernacle church, called the Church in the Woods. It was built in 1883 for the gypsies who then camped on the common and took five weeks to finish.

All Saints at East Meon is one of the best Norman churches in the south of England and has one of the seven black Tournai marble fonts that were brought back from the Continent by Bishop Henri De Blois of Winchester in the 1100s. There are four in Hampshire: another in Winchester Cathedral, one in St Mary Bourne and a fourth in St Michael's, Southampton.

A small forgotten chapel lies almost on the Berkshire border on Welshman's Road. It was built for the Countess of Huntingdon's Connexion, followers of George Whiteman and his Methodists. Many of these later became Congregational chapels.

Nately Scures Church is the smallest still in use in Hampshire and is a very rare example (only three remain in the country) of a single-cell, aisleless Norman church. It also notably has four tablet memorials in the shape of suits of playing cards.

A remarkable prefabricated church was the Crinoline Church: it was rebuilt three times in three different locations across Portsea Island. Initially erected in 1858 as a temporary church for St Bartholomew's, three and a half years later it was reconstructed to become St Simon's, near Waverley Road, Southsea. The next purchaser, in 1866, was the Admiralty and the building was dismantled again and re-erected just outside the new barracks at Eastney, its last incarnation, where it served the Royal Marines until 1905. The building was rather complex as a design for a temporary building, with twenty 'sides' and gable windows. Its roof shape quickly earned it the name the Crinoline Church after the style of dress in the same period.

Quarley Church has the unusual, nearly unique, feature (save one or two others in the country) of having its bells outside, in a cedar-shingled frame. It is mainly Norman with some Saxon features and also a rather incongruous Palladian-style east window, a very early example of its kind.

The Crinoline Church, Portsmouth, in the nineteenth century.

Silchester Church has Roman bricks visible in its walls and buttresses. Its predecessor could be the earliest-known Christian church in Britain, as this church is built within the walls of the Roman city of Calleva Atrebatum.

St Andrew's Church in Tichborne is unique in the county for having a Catholic chapel within an Anglican church, as the local noble family were strong Catholics. Its chancel has Saxon features and was probably built by Saxon craftsmen in the Norman period. It also has a tragic memorial to the young Richard Tichborne, who lived only 'one yeare six months & too daies'. It is said a gypsy laid a curse on him when refused food at the door of Tichborne House. He was to be drowned on a certain day. Thinking they would be safe from the curse up on the high downs, the boy was taken there on the day. However, he was said to have fallen from his carriage into a cart rut full of water and drowned all the same!

St Hubert's Chapel at Idsworth is picturesque in its isolation and altitude, but inside the wall paintings, dated to about 1330, are among the most beautiful and important in the county. It is thought they represent the story of St John the Baptist and St Peter and St Paul.

In St Andrew's Church at Hurstbourne Priors has a monument to Sir Robert Oxenbridge (1574) and his wife and it features kneeling figures of their twelve children, six of whom hold skulls indicating they died before their parents. A similar monument exists at Warnford Church to Sir Thomas Neale and his two wives, showing nine of his children, four carrying skulls.

The smallest church in Hampshire is at Upper Eldon on the road to Braishfield, now in a private garden (although pedestrian access is allowed). It is a single-celled Norman church cared for by the Church Preservation Trust.

Chilcomb is a small early Norman church, but so early that Saxon influence is notable, including a narrow chancel arch and a high nave.

Mattingley Church has a very unusual construction usually reserved for secular buildings. It is timber framed and infilled with red brick nogging in a herringbone fashion.

Lee-on-the-Solent is an interesting example of a modern church, completed in 1933. Its rows of curved concrete parabolic arches that make up the nave and mini-aisles give it an upturned-boat-like, cocooning feel.

Minstead is a remarkable-looking church. It looks like a house from the outside and once inside it has two extra seating galleries one on top of each other, what seems like two naves (actually one is a transept for yet more seating), a Saxon font and two private pews, with windows and a fireplace in one.

The Royal Garrison Church in Portsmouth has had an incredibly chequered history, starting as a hospital and a hostel for pilgrims in the 1200s with a hall and a chapel. It then became an ammunition store, saw the murder of the Bishop of Chichester by aggrieved seamen (see Chapter 5, Disasters), then became the governor's house, where Charles II married Katharine of Braganza in 1662 and where the heads of state of Europe met in 1814 to celebrate the defeat of Napoleon (although it turns out they were wrong). Thereafter, the nave was bombed roofless on 10 January 1941. Today, maintained by English Heritage, its story is told in its stained glass.

INTRIGUING INSCRIPTIONS

Three Heartbreakers
At St Swithun-upon-Kingsgate in Winchester is a memorial that was transferred from the demolished Church of St Maurice. Written in Latin, the translation reads:

The epitaph of the very untimely death of four infants who were both born and, alas, died again within three years. Four infants are buried in this urn, each of whom died at the threshold of its life. Jane, seeing 10 days, could be called long-lived compared with the rest if you count the time. Anna lived four days; the second Anna only lived three days; John cried out and died. Certainly, therefore, how truly they say that like the hour, the fleeting life dawns and dies away quickly. John Bond, father, MP. AD1612

Broughton Well was made in 1921 in memory of John Fripps's son, killed in 1915. The inscription reads: 'On parent knees a naked new born child, weeping thou satst while all around thee smiled. So live, that smiling in thy long last sleep, Calm thou mayst smile while all around thee weep.'

In Romsey Abbey lies a memorial to Alice Taylor, a child who died of scarlet fever in 1843. Her grief-wracked father, a doctor who couldn't save her, decided to preserve her memory with his amateur but excellent sculpture skills. She is portrayed, life-size, as if asleep on a bed with the inscription simply reading: 'Is it well with the child?' from the Bible, II Kings, Chapter 4.

Strange Stories

Thomas Eyre, an eccentric character of the early 1800s, is responsible for several inscriptions around Burley in the New Forest, but perhaps the strangest is at a house near Castle Hill that reads: 'Black bush in the Vill of Bistern Closes, Near this is the remains of a camp or castle, either of the ancient Britons, Romans or Saxons, with the Agger, Vallum, Fosse, Tumulus, or Barrows. Be Civil, quiet, and useful. T. Eyre 1823.' Presumably it refers to the Iron Age hill fort at Castle Hill. Eyre was a local benefactor and is buried in the chapel at Burley, which he helped to pay for.

Crondall Church has two inscriptions of note. Firstly, one known as the Imp memorial, a small brass with a skeleton in a shroud and the following words:

John Eager, des March XX, 1641 –
You earthly impes which here behold
This picture with your eyes
Remember the end of mortal men
And where their glory lies IE

Secondly, poor Deborah Maxwell is said to have died 'by her dress catching fire whilst her attention was engaged in writing'.

A stone monument in Harewood Forest near Longparish, called Dead Man's Plack, tells a story of intrigue, betrayal, jealousy and murder, which seems to have been par for the course in Anglo-Saxon royal families. The inscription by Lieutenant Colonel William Iremonger in 1825 tells the story that played out in the forest and nearby Wherwell:

About the Year of our Lord DCCCCLXIII Upon this Spot beyond Time of Memory. Called Deadman's Plack Tradition reports that Edgar (Surnamed the Peaceable) King of England in the ardor of Youth, Love and Indignation Slew with his own hand his Treacherous and Ungrateful Favourite Earl Athelwold owner of this Forest of Harewood in resentment of the Earl's having basely betrayed his Royal confidence and perfidiously married his Intended Bride The Beauteous Elfrida Daughter of Ordgar Earl of Devonshire afterwards Wife to King Edgar and by him Mother of King Ethelred the IInd, which Queen Elfrida after Edgar's Death murdered his eldest Son King Edward the Martyr and founded the Nunnery of Wherwell.

It's the stuff of legend, the truth of which is difficult to verify, but indeed King Edward, the boy king, was murdered at Corfe Castle in 979 and Wherwell Abbey was founded in 986 by Queen Elfrida.

The Old School House in Boldre was formerly a school and was funded from the profits of a book, *English Travellers and Italian Brigands* (1866), written by W.J.C. Moens. The plaque states: 'In thankful memory of deliverance from Brigands of the Province of Salerno in Italy by payment of a ransom of L. 1500 after 102 days captivity, in the year 1865 W.J.C. Moens of Tweed Esqre. Erected this Church of England School AD 1869.'

In Southwick there is a memorial to General Pakenham's four sons, all of whom died in places appropriate to the age of Empire: one in Lucknow, another at Fort Gwalior (India), one in the Crimean War at Inkerman 'in the fatal sandbag battery' and the last 'of decline' in the Red Sea.

Dr Francis Douce (died 1760) favoured pyramids (like his cousin, Paulet St John) and has one as his tomb at Nether Wallop churchyard. He also left money in his will 'that the boys and girls of this parish are taught to read and write and cast account in a little way, but they must not go too far least it makes them saucy and the girls all want to be chamber maids, and in a few years you will be in want of cooks'.

Thomas Thetcher was an unfortunate member of the Hampshire Militia who found himself the recipient of some lethal germs in a less-than-well-fermented beer in 1764. The inscription on his gravestone in Winchester Cathedral graveyard reminds us of the dangers of the drinking water (or weak beer made with it) at the time, and Winchester was notorious for its disgusting water supply:

Here sleeps in peace a Hampshire Grenadier
Who caught his death by drinking cold small beer
Soldiers be wise from his untimely fall
And when ye're hot drink Strong or none at all

However, the inscription detailing this incident inspired a later visitor. Bill Wilson, an American soldier, visited the grave in 1918 when he was in the county for the First World War. Years later, while suffering as an alcoholic, he remembered poor Thomas's bad choice of beer and he is mentioned as an inspiration for the *Alcoholics Anonymous Big Book*, which Wilson wrote detailing his recovery method.

FIVE SAXON CHURCHES

Corhampton has a remarkable surviving Saxon church, built in the eleventh century and little altered. It has original nave, chancel arch and north doorway, pilasters (projecting column on a wall) and 'long and short' stones at the wall corners. It can even boast an Anglo-Saxon sundial and an original altar. The wall paintings inside the church are some of the earliest and important in Hampshire and probably date to the twelfth century. They include a depiction of St Swithun mending eggs, said to be one of his miracles.

Boarhunt, on Portsdown Hill outside Portsmouth, is dated to 1064. Its narrow, plain chancel arch is typically Anglo-Saxon.

St Andrew's Church in Nether Wallop has the most remarkable wall paintings in Hampshire, part of which are Anglo-Saxon. The Christ in Majesty above the chancel arch is probably the only wall painting of its date (late tenth or early eleventh century) to still be in its original place. It is the work of the Winchester School of artists. It also has later wall paintings depicting the results of sabbath-breaking and a distinctive picture of a large bell.

The oldest bit of Saxon architecture in Hampshire is part of the church at Titchfield. Stone churches were rare in the early Anglo-Saxon period, but here the lower section of the tower, the porch, dates to around the late seventh or early eighth century (with a twelfth- or thirteenth-century tower on top).

All Hallows Church in Wickham has a rare ninth-century Saxon gravestone. It is from a tomb of, perhaps an abbess, but certainly a woman of importance. The inscription in Latin reads: 'Here lies Frithburga, buried in peace.'

SIGNS OF ROOD-NESS

Many churches used to have a rood before the reformation. It was a large crucifixion figure usually between the nave and chancel, often standing on a rood screen and sometimes covered with a decorated canopy roof. Some were carved in stone on the outside of a building. Most roods were removed or destroyed in the sixteenth century, but some signs of them remain.

There is an Anglo-Saxon rood above the porch at Breamore Church, defaced by reformers, but still with some of its painted colour. The church also has an arch with an Anglo-Saxon inscription. Inscribed perhaps over 1,000 years ago, it reads: 'HER SWUTELATH SEO GECWYDRAEDNES THE' and means: 'Here is manifested the Word to Thee.'

Headbourne Worthy is dedicated to that great Anglo-Saxon saint, Swithun. Its setting is beautiful and tranquil between paths of a stream, and it has occupied this spot for around 1,000 years, although its watery location has required some hefty restoration of the foundations. It has a rare, carved stone rood, sadly defaced during the Reformation, on the external west wall (now in the vestry), as well as Saxon pilasters and long-and-short stonework.

Romsey Abbey has two Saxon roods. One, life-size, on the outside west wall of the south transept and another smaller one in St Anne's Chapel.

St Johns, Winchester, is the oldest parish church in the city and still retains its ancient feel, with heavy Norman pillars, a rood screen and rare external staircase to it and 1200s wall paintings. It is built on top of a Roman cemetery, on the main road out of Winchester to London in medieval times.

Dummer Church has a unique-in-Hampshire rood canopy (or curved roof once above a rood) above its chancel arch, painted bright blue with gold bosses. It also has an old pulpit and gallery. The pulpit dates to 1380, making it one of the six oldest in England.

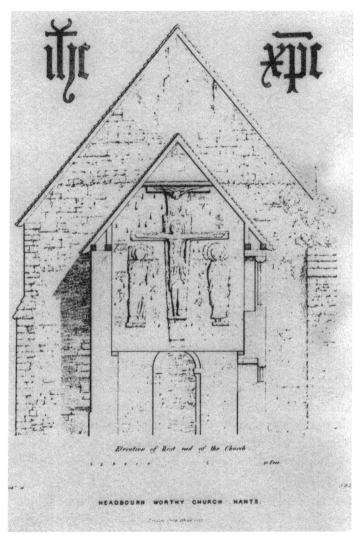

A sketch of the damaged rood on the external west wall of St Swithun's Church, Headbourne Worthy. By Owen Brown Carter in his paper on the church in Quarterly Papers on Architecture, vol. III (1845).

10

LOST AND FOUND

LOST PROPERTY

How could Hampshire have lost the bones of one of England's greatest kings? King Alfred the Great died in 899 CE. He was initially buried in the Anglo-Saxon Old Minster in Winchester. However, he was soon moved to a new church next door, New Minster, along with his wife, Alswith, and son, King Edward. But by 1110 New Minster moved to Hyde, outside the North Gate of Winchester, along with its famous graves. Come the time of King Henry VIII and the Reformation, this great monastery was destroyed and nobody thought to save the graves of our illustrious kings and queen. Later a bridewell (a prison) was built on the site and any bones found were thoughtlessly dispersed. An archaeologist, John Mellor, had a go at excavating the area in 1866 and found some bones before he was discredited. His excavated finds were later buried in St Bartholomew's Church, but dating in 2013 ruled them out as Alfred's bones. So where next? A small fragment of pelvis bone from the site of Hyde Abbey, languishing in the Winchester City Museum collection, was also dated and found to be of the right age, 895–1017 CE. As this site was only built and lived on from 1110, these would appear to be Anglo-Saxon bones brought here from an earlier grave, as Alfred and Edward would have been. So, is this small fragment all we have of Alfred or Edward, our great Kings of Wessex?

The first part of Southampton Docks, the Outer Dock, was built between 1838 and 1843 and was the beginning of the development of Southampton as the huge shipping and liner port it subsequently became. The foundation stone of this dock was laid amid great celebration: 20,000 people gathered, vessels in the harbour dressed in colours, steamers manned their yards. The stone was laid down with the following speech: 'May the Great Architect of the Universe enable us to carry on and finish the work of which we have now laid the foundation stone and every other undertaking that may tend to the advantage of the Town County of Southampton and its harbour.' The dock did flourish but the foundation stone itself was later lost. It was eventually discovered in 1900 by a group of workmen, in its original position but embedded in concrete. It was decided to raise it and inscribe it. It was indeed raised but its whereabouts then forgotten again! It was once again discovered in 1948 and placed on a plinth at Ocean Terminal, where it remained until 1983. It is now on display in the Eastern Docks, just inside Dock Gate 4.

Rather unexpectedly, in a church in the middle of the market town of Alresford can be found two stones with cruciform writing: the first stone is from the Ziggurat at the great city of Ur (modern Iraq), is dedicated to the Moon god Nannar and dates to around 2150 BCE, and the other is from King Nebuchadnezzar's Palace in Babylon from around 604–562 BCE. They were donated by the Rev. J.H. Pellatt Still in 1957.

REDISCOVERED TREASURES

White-clawed crayfish, our only native crayfish, have suffered a 95 per cent decline in the UK and were believed completely extinct in Winchester after a catastrophic plague, the last one seen in 1991. Since then the non-native signal crayfish had moved in. However, thirty years after that siting, while work was being undertaken in Winnall Moors Nature reserve in Winchester in 2022, a colony of them was found by reserve workers, hiding under tree roots. It is a mystery whether they had survived the plague and hidden undetected or had recolonised the river. The crayfish are also being conserved at other 'ark' sites across Hampshire by the Hampshire and Isle of Wight Wildlife Trust.

Otters are another animal 'found' again in Hampshire. With numbers crashing to extinction point in south-east England in the 1960s, they have now recolonised areas. In the River Itchen at Winchester, three otters were introduced in 1994. They have thrived and some have made their home at the City Mill. They even have their own Twitter account, @WCMOtters. Marsh fritillary butterflies also died out in the county in the 1990s but were reintroduced to Hampshire in 2018 and have since succeeded in establishing a colony.

George Shepherd was an artist in the early 1800s and produced wonderful watercolour depictions of Winchester and the areas around, full of contemporary figures peopling the scenes. Until recently much of his work was lost, until local book dealer and researcher Bill Hoade 'rediscovered' his work while browsing a copy of *Winchester Illustrated* in the Winchester College archives. He went on to track down dispersed work by Shepherd in London, Oxford, Middlesex, Kent and Cornwall, and found many 'lost' views by the artist. He published a history of the man and his work with over 200 illustrations he had found, *George Shepherd: His Life and Work*.

A recumbent lady (made of stone) was found buried in a field in 1820. Originally from Droxford Church, and now back there again, she had lain in the field for around 200 years having been removed at the time of the Civil War.

The great Anglo-Saxon church at Winchester, known as the Old Minster, was one of the largest and most important churches in the country, in perhaps the largest religious complex north of the Alps. It had witnessed the conversion of the West Saxon kings to Christianity, the coronation of Edward the Confessor, the funeral of Alfred the Great and many other royal spectacles. But it was demolished in 1093 when the Norman church was consecrated and its position was lost to memory. There were several theories as to where the remains of this great church were but until some of the most daring, extensive and technically challenging excavations of the twentieth century nobody knew for sure. Over several archaeological seasons in the 1960s and '70s, under the leadership of Martin Biddle and Birthe Kyolbye-Biddle, the layout was determined. Today that layout can be seen reproduced in the bricks that lie next to Winchester Cathedral, revealing it to be on a slightly different orientation to the Norman church and its west end, therefore being overlapped by the later cathedral.

MYSTERIOUS FINDS

In 1839 a coffin was found at Romsey Abbey, and when opened all that was found was a finger bone that crumbled into dust and a whole head of female hair with a plait over 45cm long. Whose was this? Was it one of the Saxon abbesses and saints, Merewenna or Ethelfleada? It was not until 2016 that more information came to light. Radio carbon dating did indeed place it between 965 and 1045 CE, so Anglo-Saxon, and its position and lead coffin would suggest a nun of the monastery of some importance. The mystery of who it was and why a scalp and hair would be preserved remain, though.

More coffins were opened when the mortuary chests of Winchester Cathedral were analysed in 2012–19. Therein rest the bones of many Anglo-Saxon and Norman kings, bishops and one queen. The bones of two mysterious, previously unrecorded, boys were found, aged between 10 and 15, dating to the eleventh

One of the mortuary chests, containing bones of Norman and Saxon kings and bishops, as displayed on the quire screens in Winchester Cathedral.

to twelfth centuries. They are assumed to be of royal blood, as they were found with the other royal bones, but who are they? Was there foul play? The mystery remains.

TWO RE-FOUND HOARDS

Hoards are groups of objects buried by their original owners for a number of purposes – to protect them, store them or sacrifice them. Some were never recovered until curious people began digging centuries later. The Winchester Hoard is the most important to be discovered in Hampshire. Discovered in 2000 near Winchester, it has two sets of Iron Age (about 75 BCE) gold jewellery, each with a necklace torc, two gold brooches held together by a chain and two gold bracelets. A total of 1,160g of very pure gold was used to make the objects. One of the torcs is bigger than the other, possibly because one was made for a man and the other for a woman. The necklaces were crafted differently from other torcs made in Britain at this time, utilising Roman jewellery-making techniques, so it is possible that a Roman craft worker made them and they were a diplomatic gift from the Roman world to leaders in Britain. This was only the third discovery of its kind in Britain, and one of fewer than a dozen from northern Europe. It is now in the British Museum.

A most unusual hoard of 7,083 forged French coins, dated 1711, was found at Bishop's Waltham in 2012 under the floorboards of a shop. They were thirty Deniers 'Mousquetaire' colonials, coins distributed in large quantities in New France, Louisiana and the French West Indies. After analysis they were found to be counterfeit coins, though. Why the coins ended up in Bishop's Waltham and not in America is a mystery. One theory is that they may have been stolen by a French sailor and hidden until he could return from his voyage to the New World. Or perhaps the owner realised they were fake and deposited them as having no value? Or perhaps there was foul play – were the English attempting to infiltrate the French economy? Many of the coins were preserved by the Portable Antiquities Scheme, and the British Museum sold the remainder of the hoard to a London coin company, who in turn sold them to Mid-American Rare Coin Galleries and Texas Numismatic Investments Inc. So it took a little longer than expected, actually over 300 years, for this shipment of 'Mousquetaires' to make it to the New World!

PIECES OF HAMPSHIRE
NOT IN HAMPSHIRE

The British Museum in London holds many treasures of Hampshire, including: a Roman sandstone altar found in Jewry Street, Winchester, dedicated to the mother goddesses of Britain, Germany and Italy; Roman mosaics from Thruxton and Abbotts Ann; fossils collected by Gustav Brander near Barton and described in his ground-breaking book *Fossilia Hantoniensis*; and the Winchester Hoard (Rm 50).

Hampshire lost parts of the body of its mega-saint, Swithun, with relics travelling as far afield as France and Norway. After being ignominiously moved inside the Old Minster in 974, the body was divided, with some bones being kept on the High Altar and some being put in a reliquary in a chapel at the front of the church. Bishop Alphege decided to bring Swithun's head to Canterbury when he was promoted in 1006, but it was later given to Evreux in Normandy. An arm was given to Peterborough and a second arm was taken to a church in Stavanger, Norway, in the 1100s by a Reinhald. Even the rest of the surely-by-now-scanty remains were lost in 1538 when his shrine in the cathedral was broken apart by Henry VIII's reforming men.

In 1974, Hampshire lost Christchurch and Bournemouth to Dorset, with the reorganisation of local governments. It was considered that the urban centre of Bournemouth could be taken into Dorset, which didn't have any, and out of Hampshire, which already had lots. In 1895 the parish of Combe was transferred to Berkshire, removing the highest point of Hampshire, Walbury Hill, to that county. The highest point had to be transferred to Pilot Hill, the next one along. However, Hampshire gained a section near Martin, in the far west, from Wiltshire.

Several historic buildings from Hampshire, in danger of demolition, were dismantled and reconstructed at the Weald and Downland Museum, in West Sussex, which preserves vernacular architecture. A little bit of Hampshire can be seen there today: the Hall House from Boarhunt (1355–90), a brick-drying shed (1733) from Petersfield, a treadwheel for a well from Catherington (late seventeenth century), Court Barn from Lee-on-the-Solent (late seventeenth century), the Market Hall from Titchfield (sixteenth century) and a tin tabernacle church from South Wonston (1908).

The archaeological finds from the great Iron Age settlement and Roman city at Silchester are all over the border in Reading Museum, Berkshire.

Bricks from a Lyndhurst farmhouse can be found at the Royal Botanic Gardens in Sydney, Australia. They were taken from the only remaining wall of Vernalls, the Lyndhurst house of Admiral Arthur Philip, the founder of Sydney and governor of New South Wales. Some 6,000 bricks, weighing 15 tons, were shipped to Australia, some in the ships re-enacting the voyage of the first fleet in 1987. These were to be distributed in various memorials including the Botanic Gardens, as well as in Heritage Square, Gordon, New South Wales, and in Kable Connections Library at Lyndhurst.

Miss England I, the boat built at Hythe that beat the world water speed record in 1928, is now in the Science Museum. *Miss Britain III*, the world record-breaking power boat made by Hubert Scott-Paine's British Power Boat Company at Hythe, is in the National Maritime Museum, Greenwich.

The *Liber Vitae* is a book a monastery would hold listing all the people who have helped the monastery and done good works in its life. Usually full of monks, abbots and lay patrons, these people are guaranteed a place in heaven. There are only a handful in existence but Hyde Abbey in Winchester has a wonderful one detailing the life of this medieval institution. It lists the relics held by the abbey (including the head of St Valentine and the arm of St Vincent, and the crown of thorns apparently) and its estates. It has an illustration of King Cnut and Queen Emma giving a gold cross to the monastery. It is now in the British Library along with the *Benedictional of St Aethelwold* and *Bald's Leechbook*, other religious books of the 900s featuring classic illumination in the Winchester School style.

LOST HAMPSHIRE LANDMARKS

The great Ocean Terminal at Southampton Docks would have been known not just to Hampshire people but to all those who entered and exited the country via the great liners of the twentieth century. Southampton had been a port for the great Atlantic liners since the 1890s, but it was only in 1948 that Southampton Docks built its incredible art deco passenger terminal – the Ocean Terminal cost £750,000, was 395m long and 34m wide. Its visitors' balcony extended the whole length of the building and it had a rail line that connected directly to it. On the upper floor were two large passenger lounges, with refreshment buffet, telephones, banking facilities and customs halls, all finished with uplighting, art deco details and burred wood panelling. You could embark and disembark directly from the lounges via a hydraulic telescopic gangway. It was a wonderful addition to the great age of transatlantic travel, albeit towards the end of its heyday. It was demolished in 1983. A new terminal greets the cruise ships of today, albeit not with the mid-century panache of the original.

Portsmouth's Tricorn Centre was built in the mid-1960s in the Brutalist style as a shopping centre, was voted the most hated building in the UK by Radio 4 listeners in 2001 and was demolished in 2004. It had two pubs and a nightclub that hosted acts such as Marc Bolan, Slade and Status Quo. But it became more and more seedy and the location of suicide attempts due to its height. The Prince of Wales called it 'a mildewed lump of elephant droppings', although it was loved when first built and others tried to get it listed in order to rescue it. Essayist Jonathan

Meades commented: 'You don't go knocking down Stonehenge or Lincoln Cathedral. I think buildings like the Tricorn were as good as that. They were great monuments of an age.'

Winchester Castle was built high up on Winchester's West Hill early in 1067 by William the Conqueror and was one of the strongest fortresses in the country. The Battle of Hastings was won but the principal city of the Anglo-Saxon kings needed controlling. A huge square tower was built, replaced by round towers in the 1200s, and dominated the city until 1659, when it was razed to the ground on Oliver Cromwell's orders. The Great Hall remains today, where kings and queens of England held their courts, parliaments, hosted feasts, celebrated Easter, Whitsun or Christmas and 'wore their crowns'. A huge but unfinished royal palace was built on the castle site for King Charles II by Sir Christopher Wren in 1683, to be an English Versailles. But it was never used as a royal residence as the king died and it burnt down in 1894.

Southampton Castle, an early Norman castle with its own quay, was restored in 1286. It had the sea on two sides and a moat, and seven gates and towers at the corners. It commanded the rivers Itchen and Test, and Southampton Water. It fell into disrepair and the stones were used to repair the city walls. Later a Gothic recreation of a castle was built by the Marquis of Lansdowne there but it too was demolished in 1818. Today the apartment block Castle House marks the spot.

Netley Hospital was a vast military hospital built on the waterfront of Southampton Water in 1856 for the Crimean War and highly visible by the troop ships passing by on Southampton Water. It was a quarter of a mile long (some say patients were later occasionally transported by jeep down the long corridors) with its own gasworks, reservoir, school, stables, bakery and prison. There was a grand officers' mess, complete with ballroom, and a small natural history museum including elephant skulls – just the sort of thing you wanted to see after returning from a theatre of war. There was even a salty swimming pool, fed by a windmill pumping water from the sea. But even this mighty medical edifice couldn't cope with the industrialised warfare of the First World War, during which three trains a day arrived with the wounded including German prisoners of war. It had the first purpose-built military asylum, known as D Block. Here men suffering shellshock were treated – or perhaps locked away in padded cells. Soldiers from all over the world were brought here: Aboriginal Australians, Maoris and black South Africans, and one floor was given over to Indian troops. In the hospital grounds, a concrete platform, or ghat, was built at the side of a stream for cremations and the ashes were tipped into the stream, perhaps to join the Ganges one day. After D-Day the hospital was kept very busy, receiving 400 casualties on 11 June 1944, with 141 operations carried out in one thirty-six-hour period. It was demolished in 1966 and the only remaining section, the chapel and cupola, form the backdrop to the Royal Victoria Country Park.

Fawley, on the west side of Southampton Water, is home to both a huge oil refinery and a disused power station with a nearly 200m chimney, both could be seen from all over the New Forest and from Southampton Water. The massive chimney of the power station was brought down in one big explosion on 31 October 2021. The power station had been used as a location in several films: in *Mission Impossible: Rogue Nation*, as a Moroccan power station; and as an imperial shipyard on the planet Corellia in *Solo: A Star Wars Story*.

FADED SPAS

At Alverstoke, near Gosport, the Regency houses of the Crescent and the small pump house were to have been the start of a spa upon the discovery of beneficial properties in the local water.

Rumour has it that this idea was dropped when this was found to be the result of sewage contamination!

Southsea in Portsmouth was little more than heathland, called the Great Morass until the nineteenth century when a Mr Croxton began turning it into a seaside resort named Croxton Town. It soon became Southsea, after Southsea Castle nearby, and marketed itself as Sunny Southsea. Due to its southerly location and shelter from northerly winds by Portsdown Hill, Southsea enjoys one of the mildest winters in the United Kingdom, and experiences higher temperatures and higher sunshine hours than areas surrounding it, so perhaps it is Sunny Southsea! Clarence Pier was built to board steamers to the Isle of Wight but soon became a seaside pier with a pavilion and a concert hall. Southsea also had a pump rooms by 1816, and vapour baths, showers, card playing and assembly rooms.

In 1860, Blondin, the famous tightrope walker, who crossed Niagara Falls, came to Southsea. He crossed a tightrope strung across the large tea gardens of the Clarence Tavern. He astounded the spectators by pushing a wheelbarrow across the rope and pausing midway to enjoy refreshment, while still balanced!

Caroline, the Princess of Wales, bathed in the sea during her stay at Emsworth in 1805 and for some time the town thought it might become a royal watering place. A bathing house was built with seawater baths and heating facilities. It is now the Emsworth Sailing Club.

A pier with its own railway and tower once made Lee-on-the-Solent a candidate for the next Bournemouth, however it was not to be and there is no trace of all three now, the tower being demolished in 1968. Only the station building survives as an amusement arcade.

Barton-on-Sea's wonderful sea breezes were recognised from 1888 onwards with the coming of the railway to New Milton. Taking advantage of the magnificent sea views, a grand hotel was built, the Barton Court Hotel, and large houses, other hotels and a golf course on the clifftop followed. Two of Barton's hotels became military convalescent homes during the First World War, utilising the fresh seaside air for recovery. Golf and the seaside air can still be enjoyed today but Barton on Sea never had a pier or promenade as an estate agent's advert of 1904 shows, perhaps an aspiration never realised!

Milford-on-Sea was promoted by local landowner William Cornwallis-West as a seaside resort (see A History of Hampshire Through Williams in Chapter 7, Hampshire People) but lack of funds and an unfortunate outbreak of typhoid put off potential visitors. However, Milford remains a beautiful seaside spot to visit today.

As you pass the scrap metal sites and huge container ships at Southampton it is hard to credit it as a place of health-giving waters. However, Southampton had a brief period as a seaside

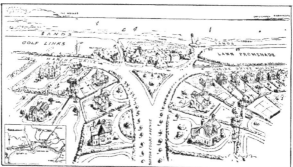

A 1904 advertisement by an estate agent for plots at Barton-on-Sea, showing an 'aspirational' promenade and pier. (Courtesy Milton Heritage Society)

resort and spa town from around 1750 to 1812, after Frederick Prince of Wales came to Southampton for a day and bathed in the sea on the western shore. Nobility followed, genteel houses were built (Gloucester Square, Brunswick Square and Albion Place) and fortuitously a spring was suddenly found providing health giving spa water near modern-day Portland Terrace. There was never much of a beach but there were seawater baths (filled by the tide), a theatre, bathing machines on the West Quay, the Long Rooms, with ballroom and card rooms, and a promenade called The Beach, giving views of the water. An ill-fated scheme called the Polygon to provide a Bath-like crescent of houses ended in bankruptcy, however. By 1812 royalty had transferred their affections to Brighton and Southampton's spa credentials dwindled.

DISCONNECTED GRAVEYARDS

Chilton Candover had a Norman church, which was pulled down in 1878 and a new one built. However, the vicar began excavating the old church on the basis of a remark of an old man in the village, who said that as a boy he used to go under the old church and kick skulls around! The vicar found a rare Norman crypt, forgotten for fifty years. The old village, however, is still lost under the field next to the church. In 1562, the new owner of the manor, John Fisher, had destroyed the village, leaving only the church.

Otterbourne Church once stood in the older part of the village and today you can see the old graveyard on the Otterbourne to Colden Common road, Kiln Lane. A new church was built further west by novelist Charlotte Yonge's father, William Yonge.

On top of Hordle Cliff lie the remains of a graveyard. One might surmise the church had fallen into the sea by erosion. However, this is not true, the church was removed a mile or two north to Hordle in 1830. Some graves are of shipwreck victims washed ashore here.

St Giles graveyard stands alone with no church just off the Alresford Road in Winchester. It used to have a church in the Middle Ages and this and the graveyard served the Nova Villa or New Town that grew up on St Giles Hill to house the Fair of St Giles. The graveyard is the only surviving part. It is managed for wildlife now and is a mysterious and beautiful spot.

In East Stratton, the church was demolished in 1887 and a new one built to the north of the village. A stone cross marks the spot where it once stood and parch marks in hot summers show the ghostly outline of the old church. However, the high water table precluded burials at this site and coffins were transported over a mile to Micheldever along a 'burying road'.

GARDENS THAT HAVE LOST THEIR HOUSES

Paultons Park, now a theme park including Peppa Pig World, but once a grand Capability Brown landscape, can be found near Romsey. Its house became derelict after 1954 and eventually burnt down in 1963.

Leigh Park, near Havant, still retains its surrounding estate, open as a park, with a handful of remaining follies and a lake. However, only a supporting arcade of a terrace and a separate library building (see Isolated Octagons) remain of the three houses that once dominated it.

Basing House, when first built in 1535, was said to be the largest private house in the country, with 360 rooms. Stormed by Oliver Cromwell, ransacked and razed after an exhausting and long Civil War siege, only the ruins remain next to the walled garden set out in Jacobean style.

At Warnford Park, the park is open for snowdrop walks in February and the church is inside the park gates. It has a dower house (or bath house) in the 'Strawberry Hill' Gothic style and the ruins of a thirteenth-century house behind the church, but no large house: following decline after the Second World War, it was demolished in 1958.

MISSING MONASTERIES

Not many counties could boast so long and so strong a history of monastic life. At the time of the Dissolution of the Monasteries (between 1536 and 1539) Hampshire had thirteen, five of them ancient foundations with an Anglo-Saxon heritage, including three at Winchester (Priory of St Swithun, Hyde Abbey and St Mary's Abbey or Nunnaminster). Others were Beaulieu, Netley, Hartley Wintney, St Denys, Breamore, Southwick, Mottisfont, Titchfield, Romsey and Wherwell. As landlords, the monasteries owned about a quarter of Hampshire manors and 261 monks and nuns lived there. Where did the monasteries go? Actually, if you play detective there's more of them about than you might think.

You can find three of them still in use:

- Winchester Cathedral was the abbey church of the Priory of St Swithun.
- Romsey Abbey church was bought by the townspeople for £100 and turned into the (huge) parish church.
- The abbey refectory at Beaulieu Abbey was turned into the new parish church.

Others were turned into Tudor country houses by their new owners: Mottisfont; Titchfield; Netley; and Breamore.

Lead from the roofs and windows was melted down, sold and went to the king's coffers, as were the tiles and timber:

- Stone from Beaulieu Abbey went to build Cowes and Calshot Castle.
- Lead from St Mary's went to build Hurst Castle.
- Stone from Netley built a small castle at Netley itself.

- In Winchester the abbey buildings acted as a stone source for over a century. Stone was used from St Mary's for Symonds Almshouses (on Symonds Street) in 1608, and Hyde Abbey stones can be seen in houses and walls at Hyde. Community archaeological digs run by Hyde 900 unearth more pieces of the abbey each year, often in people's back gardens.

One final monastery really was founded and then lost, to the sea. Hayling Priory had been founded in Anglo-Saxon times but was inundated by the sea in the early 1300s. It was dissolved by its mother house, the Abbey of Jumieges, in 1413 but then some say (although not all historians agree) the site was dissolved in another way, becoming drowned and forgotten under the sea off Hayling Island.

SELECTED BIBLIOGRAPHY

GENERAL

Barton, J., *Hidden Hampshire* (Newbury: Countryside Books, 1989).

Beaumont James, T., 'The Black Death in Hampshire', *Hampshire Papers,* No. 18, 1999.

Biddle, M., *The Search for Winchester's Anglo-Saxon Minsters* (Oxford: Winchester Excavations Committee, 2018).

Boogaart, Pieter, *A272: An Ode to a Road* (London: Pallas Athene, 2000).

Bryan, D., Buchanan, G., Dixon, C. and King J., *Bloody British History Winchester* (Stroud: The History Press, 2013).

Berthon Boat Company Ltd, 'Berthon History', www.berthon. co.uk/about-berthon/berthon-history/#tab3Tab

Carpenter Turner, B., *A History of Hampshire* (Oxford: University Printing House, 1978).

Cunliffe, B. (ed.), *Heywood Sumner's Wessex* (Wimborne: Roy Gasson Associates, 1985).

Davison, M., Currie, I. and Ogley, B., *The Hampshire and Isle of Wight Weather Book* (Westerham: Froglets Publications, 1993).

Defoe, D., *A Tour through the Whole of Great Britain (1724– 26).*

Draper, J., *Hampshire: The Complete Guide* (Wimborne: The Dovecote Press, 1990).

Fielding, S., *Hanged at Winchester* (Stroud: The History Press, 2010).

Fox, I., *Hampshire Tales of Mystery & Murder* (Newbury: Countryside Books, 2001).

Hare, J., 'The Dissolution of the Monasteries in Hampshire', *Hampshire Papers,* No. 16, 1999.

Hinds, K., *50 Finds from Hampshire: Objects from the Portable Antiquities Scheme* (Stroud: Amberley Publishing, 2017).

Holland, A.J., *Ships of British Oak: The Rise and Decline of Wooden Shipbuilding in Hampshire* (Newton Abbot: David & Charles, 1971).

Legg, P., *Folklore of Hampshire* (Stroud: The History Press, 2010).

Locke, S., 'George Marston: Shackleton's Antarctic Artist', *Hampshire Papers*, No. 19, 2000.

Millson, C., *Tales of Old Hampshire* (Newbury: Countryside Books, 1987).

Moody, B., *150 Years of Southampton Docks* (Southampton: Kingfisher Railway Productions, 1988).

Mowl T. & Whitaker, J., *The Historic Gardens of England: Hampshire* (Bradford-on-Avon: Stephen Morris, 2016).

National Motor Museum, *National Motor Museum* (Beaulieu: Montagu Ventures Ltd, 2003).

Rance, Adrian B., *Sea Planes and Flying Boats of the Solent* (Southampton: Southampton University Industrial Archaeology Group/Southampton City Museums, 1981).

Robinson, S., *In Black and White: The stories of and stories from one of the world's oldest newspapers* (Winchester: Jacob & Johnson Ltd, no date).

Shurlock, B. 'The Worthys and the caravan industry', *Worthy History*, No. 25, 2020.

Smith, G., *Hampshire and Dorset Shipwrecks* (Newbury: Countryside Books, 1995).

Solent Sky Aviation Museum, *Souvenir Guide Book* (Southampton: Solent Sky, 2014).

Spence, M., 'Hampshire and Australia, 1783–1801: Crime and Transportation', *Hampshire Papers*, No. 2, 1992.

Thornhill, P. and Withers, A., *Heroes and Villains of Winchester Cathedral* (Winchester: Friends of Winchester Cathedral, no date).

WEBSITES

Agincourt 600, www.agincourt600.com/agincourt-places

Associated British Ports, Southampton Tides, www.southamptonvts.co.uk/Port_Information/Navigation/Hydrography/Southampton_Tides

BBC Local Hampshire, www.bbc.co.uk/hampshire/content/image_galleries/dday_gallery.shtml?2

British Library, www.bl.uk/collection-items/balds-leechbook, www.bl.uk/collection-items/thomas-malorys-le-morte-darthur

Butterfly Conservation, butterfly-conservation.org/butterflies/duke-of-burgundy

Digital Panopticon, 'Convict Hulks', www.digitalpanopticon.org/Convict_Hulks

Farringdon ancient yew, www.ancienttreeforum.org.uk/farringdon-ancient-yew-fundraising-campaign-all-saints-hampshire

Hampshire Archives and Local Studies, hampshirearchivesandlocalstudies.wordpress.com

Hampshire Cultural Trust, collections.hampshireculture.org.uk

Hampshire History, www.hampshire-history.com

Hampshire and Isle of Wight Wildlife Trust, www.hiwwt.org.uk

Hampshire Mills, www.hampshiremills.org

Portsmouth History Centre, librariesandarchives.portsmouth.gov.uk/archive-service-and-history-centre

Royal Victoria Military Hospital, documents.hants.gov.uk/rvc/
    royal-victoria-hospital-short-history.pdf
Smugglers Britain, 'Guide Book: Southern England',
    smuggling.co.uk/gazetteer_s.html
Solent Sky Museum, www.solentsky.org
Sotonopaedia, sotonopedia.wikidot.com
Southampton Archives, www.southampton.gov.uk/arts-
    heritage/southampton-archives The Mayflower, www.
    mayflower400uk.org
Victoria County History, www.victoriacountyhistory.ac.uk

HAMPSHIRE PLACES AND
HISTORY SOCIETIES

Alresford, alresfordmemories.wordpress.com
East Meon, www.eastmeonhistory.net
East Stratton, 'History of the Church and Chapel', www.
    eaststratton.com/history-of-the-church
Emsworth Museum, emsworthmuseum.org.uk
Gosport, www.gosportsociety.co.uk/Gosport_Society_
    heritage.html
Hamble, www.hamblehistory.org.uk
Lymington, www.lymingtonharbour.co.uk/history-of-
    lymington#:~:text=From%20the%20Middle%20Ages%20
    until,some%20of%20the%20water%20evaporated
Lymington and District Historical Society, www.
    lymingtonanddistricthistoricalsociety.co.uk
Milton Heritage Society, miltonheritagesociety.co.uk
Portsmouth, www.memorialsinportsmouth.co.uk
Portsmouth Historic Dockyard Historic Trust,
    portsmouthdockyard.org.uk/timeline

Silchester, www.english-heritage.org.uk/visit/places/silchester-roman-city-walls-and-amphitheatre/history/description

The New Forest, www.newforestnpa.gov.uk

The Spring, Havant, thespring.co.uk/heritage/local-history-booklets

Worthys Local History Society, www.worthyhistory.org

The destination for history
www.thehistorypress.co.uk